B's & A's in 30 Days

Strategies for Better Grades in College

Eric Jensen, M.A.
Illustrated by Tom Kerr

BARRON'S

Many thanks to Melissa Fraser for editing

All inquiries should be addressed to:
Barron's Educational Series, Inc.
250 Wireless Boulevard
Hauppauge, New York 11788

Library of Congress Catalog Card No. 96-21840

International Standard Book No. 0-8120-9582-0

Library of Congress Cataloging-in-Publication Data
Jensen, Eric.
 B's and A's in 30 days / by Eric Jensen ; illustrated by Tom
Kerr.
     p.   cm.
 Includes bibliographical references (p.   ) and index.
 ISBN 0-8120-9582-0
 1. Study skills. 2. Speed reading. I. Kerr, Tom, ill.
II. Title
LB2395.J428   1996
378.1'7'02812—dc20   96-21840
                                                      CIP

PRINTED IN THE UNITED STATES OF AMERICA

9 8 7 6 5 4 3 2

Contents

*The New Surefire Student Success System
for Better Grades, Less Stress, and
Greater Self-Confidence*

CAST OF CHARACTERS

INTRODUCTION

With all the books on study skills, learn to learn, and grade improvement, why one more? There are three unique qualities in this 30-day program. First, it integrates academic skills and life skills based on the newest brain research on learning. Second, it has been tested by more than 20,000 students around the world. You can be confident that it can work for you, too. And last, this unique 30-day format provides a structured daily "learning menu" for an entire month. That means you can relax and enjoy the daily brain food with confidence knowing you are managing your educational needs.

This book will work for you. All you have to do is follow directions. In 30 days you can be a confident and skilled learner ready for more than just better grades. You can be ready to take on the challenges of the 21st century's information age. If you're ready to succeed, go ahead to the next page.

GETTING B'S AND A'S

Question:

Can You Really Get B's and A's in Just 30 Days?

Answer:

Yes!

Your Path to Success Starts Here.

To Begin Day 1,
Turn the Page!

Day 1

HOW TO GET STARTED RIGHT AWAY

Congratulations! You have chosen *B's and A's in 30 Days*—a proven, user-friendly grade booster. This exciting learn-to-learn system builds self-confidence, motivation, and helps improve your grades, too. It's guaranteed to make improving your grades fun!

Today's chapter, like most of the others, will take you 30 minutes or less to read and apply to your studies. Do only what each chapter asks you to do. This lets your mind take in daily chunks of information at a rate at which they can be implemented. Too little information and you get bored. Too much and you may get overwhelmed. The success of this program depends on you following directions. Do that and you'll succeed, guaranteed. After you read each item, check it off, so you'll know what you've completed. Use this book as a tool—write in it and highlight the parts that appeal to you.

Why Use This Program?

1. You deserve good grades.
2. You want to invest just the right amount of time to succeed.

3. You know that grades help you make it in "the system."
4. You know that some students (the experts) have a system.
5. You know if you're not succeeding, you're not stupid. It's most likely that you either learn differently or don't have a success system.
6. Use this program because *it works!*

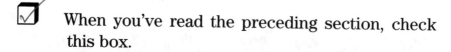 When you've read the preceding section, check this box.

What Makes This Program so Successful?

1. It's easy to use.
2. It takes just 30 days.
3. It is based on the latest brain research.
4. You can stop and start it at any time or simply go nonstop.
5. It integrates academic and life skills.
6. It's been tested by more than 20,000 students.
7. *It works!*

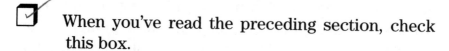 When you've read the preceding section, check this box.

How Do You Use This Program?

1. Browse through the entire book first; take five to ten minutes.
2. Set a personal goal of when you want to start and finish your next 30 days. The upcoming Monday may be best.

3. Start with the first day's chapter. Read and apply it.
4. Do one chapter a day for 30 days.
5. If you miss a day, just pick up where you left off.
6. Apply what you learn to your college work and your life at home.
7. Enjoy the success—you can plan on B's and A's in 30 days!

☑ When you've read the preceding section, check this box.

STARTING POINTS

Figure out where you are right now. We'll be setting goals tomorrow, but for now, let's get a real fix on your grades. Please fill out the next section.

Name of Class (By its title)	Most Recent Quiz/Test (Within last 30 days)	Expected Grade (At course end)	Desired Grade (At course end)
College Success Strategies		A	A

Now, use this information to fill in the blanks on the next two lines.

Total number of classes ___1___
Number of B's & A's ___1___

☑ When you've read the preceding section, check this box.

PERSONAL PROFILE

Here, all you do is two things. Tell the truth and circle your answer. Use 1 as the low end and 10 as the highest score.

On a scale of 1–10, how much do you like school? Circle your answer.

1	2	3	4	5	6	7	8	9	10
zip		low	average		not bad		good		excellent

What's your skill level in study skills and reading? Circle your answer.

1	2	3	4	5	6	7	8	9	10
zip		low	average		not bad		good		excellent

What are your confidence and self-esteem levels? Circle your answer.

1	2	3	4	5	6	7	8	9	10
zip		low	average		not bad		good		excellent

How do you rate your chances of finishing college? Circle your answer.

1	2	3	4	5	6	7	8	9	10
zip		low	average		not bad		good		excellent

Overall, how would you rate the way your coursework is going? Circle your answer.

1	2	3	4	5	6	7	8	9	10
zip		low	average		not bad		good		excellent

Great! You know where you are now. Before we finish up the day (remember, this will take 30 minutes or less every day), there's one more thing to do.

PHOTOFLASH SNEAK PREVIEW

For the next 30 days, you'll be learning something new each day. There are a lot of ideas, knowledge, and skills you can learn. But instead of overwhelming your brain with them all at once, we'll give your brain sneak previews well in advance. And instead of trying to recall everything you've learned every single day, we'll do simple reviews.

One of the easiest ways to do this is to use the photoflash method of scanning. The way this works is easy. You merely take a look at each page for the shortest length of time you can (like a photoflash). Let your brain absorb as much or as a little as naturally happens in that time. Simply turn the page, glance at it for one second or less, then look at the next page. Scan it for one second or less, then go to the next

PHOTOFLASH

page. Use a relaxed, soft focus with your eyes, purposely *not* trying to read anything. Just glance at it like you would a picture. At one second per page, this entire book (all 30 chapters) will go very quickly.

This will give your brain an early exposure to material you'll be getting later on. It is like a quick commercial on TV. The first time it's on, you may not buy the product. But, over time, the repeated message can change your buying habits.

While you'll be taking in very little information from each page on the first day, expect to be taking in much more by mid-course. By the end of the course, this same daily exercise becomes a powerful and fast daily review. Go ahead and photoflash every page in this book.

 When you're finished, check this box.

Review

Once you have finished this, your Day 1 assignment is done. Hooray! Before you move on to something else, let's review what you accomplished.

✓ You made the decision to begin the program.
✓ You read the check-in statement.
✓ You determined your present situation.
✓ You took some personal inventory.
✓ You photoflashed the whole 30-day program.
✓ You read your review for the day (that's this list).

Congratulations! You have completed the first of your 30 days to B's and A's. Close the book and we'll see you tomorrow!

Day 2

SETTING GOALS

Why set goals? Your brain responds to two commands: you can tell it *what* you want and *why* it has to do it. For example, why is it that a 100-pound woman can, in an emergency, by herself, pick up the end of a car that has stopped on her son's leg? She has a *what* (to lift the car) and a really strong *why* (to save the life of her son).

She doesn't ask herself *how* she'll do it—*she just does it!* If the *what* and *why* are strong enough, your brain will always figure out a *how*. Your goals must be clear, specific, and positive. Here's a perfect example: My goal is to get at least five B's and A's in my classes within 30 days. OK, tell that to your brain now!

First Easy Step

In the space below, write your goals for school. Make them specific, positive, and in the present tense—as if they're already being achieved. Write your goals in the spaces provided for every class. An example might be: "In English 101, I am getting an A!"

Course Grade	Sentence with Your Goal
College Success Strategies	
	"I am getting an A"

OK, time to reinforce! Write a reminder note that states your goals simply. Post it where you study. You will feed your brain the message that you want—that you expect to get and are getting—B's and A's in 30 days!

  When you've read the preceding section, check this box.

BELIEVE IT OR NOT

Beliefs—the things you hold as true—are powerful motivators. Think how fast you could swim if you really believed a shark was after you. It wouldn't matter if there was a shark or not—your belief alone would frighten you enough to get you moving fast!

Guess what? The same thing happens in school! If you believed somehow that you would get a thousand dollars in cash if you got good grades, you'd get good grades. And similarly, if you believed that a thousand

GET THOSE GRADES

dollars would be subtracted from your bank account every time your grades dipped below B, you'd do anything you could to get good grades. The point is this: those things don't really have to be true. If you believe that they are true, the effect is the same. If you believe that you can get B's and A's, it will be easier to study and you'll be more likely to get those grades!

First Easy Step

First, fill in the blanks to complete these statements:

1. I think studying is ___*necessary*___.

2. I know I can get ___*above average*___ grades.

3. I think of myself as a ___*good*___ student.

Now, look at what you've written. This tells a lot about your beliefs. Beliefs can be negative or positive. Neutral beliefs are rare. Let's look at some positive beliefs: You might believe that, "Studying is easy, fun, I can do it, it's a piece of cake, it is important to do, and it is the key to my success." You might also believe in yourself so much you say, "I know I can get top grades." And what kind of a student are you? You are the kind of student, most likely, that you believe yourself to be.

If your original answers to these three statements weren't very positive, go back and change them to positive beliefs. Now write out your three new beliefs on the next page. For example, "I am smart and talented." If you don't think they're true, make up a reason for them to be true. Really believe them. Read them to yourself every day for a week, starting today. Ready? Now do it!

1. _I am Smart and talented_
2. _I am a good problem Solver_
3. _I am dedicated._

GRADE BOOSTERS

To do the job right in school, you need the right tools. Learning is a skilled profession, and it takes tools just like a doctor, carpenter, electrician, or plumber requires tools. Some of the tools you need for good grades are

♦ access to a computer (borrow, buy, rent, or check at the library). Learn a simple word-processing software like MS Word or WordPerfect. It will serve you for years. And it sure makes assignments easier.

♦ a good filing system. Get file folders, labels for them, and a container to hold them. Many successful students like those brown accordion file holders. It reduces stress because you'll always know where your papers are.

♦ tools for writing: pens and highlighters for note-taking, an erasable pen, lots of paper, and a calculator.

Research the Professor Before You Take a Class

Sometimes you don't get a choice of classes and professors; other times, you do. Better to take a class with a great professor than take a class in a great subject. When you get a good professor, even a so-called hard subject comes alive and you'll learn more. Ask your friends. Ask other faculty members about the professors who are passionate about their subject. If you get a boring professor or one with a poor reputation, switch classes if possible.

In Class, Sit Up and Lean Forward

Never miss a class unless it's really necessary. Be on time or a bit early. Sit somewhere in the first few rows of the class. You'll be able to see everything better, including videos, overheads, a chalkboard, or demonstrations. It's less embarrassing to ask questions when you're right up close. Sit away from anyone who might be a distraction. Sitting up front not only keeps you more engaged in the class, but the professor may feel you are more interested in the subject.

Get Organized

It's easy to let yourself become disorganized when you're taking many courses. To avoid this, organize a notebook with colored tab dividers. Have a section of your notebook (maybe it's the back) that is *just for writing down assignments*. Set up a daily to do list. Add to it and check it off each day. Plan out your weekly test schedules. You know how detailed you need to make them. If an exact time for each daily to do gets you to do it, use a daily schedule. If not, simply list the item to do each day on your calendar. Use a brown accordion file organizer for loose or miscellaneous papers. Keep it alphabetized or sorted by class.

Aim for Early Success

Do whatever it takes to get a top grade on the first two tests. Over-prepare and over-study. Study smarter, not harder. Use all of the study tools in this program. If possible, make this book your study bible for the first month of a semester. When you start off strong, you create a strong first impression with the professor, you are often more motivated to learn, and you develop a positive attitude toward your courses.

Build Relationships

Building a good relationship with your professors is *not* about being a brown-noser or teacher's pet. It is about people. By knowing the professor, you begin to understand not just *what* the professor knows, but just as importantly, *how* the professor knows it. Professors often get into the teaching profession because they love the subject. For others, they value the contact with their students. If you sense your professor is a people person, be friendly. Smile a lot. Stay in class until the very end of each session.

If you miss a class, get the notes from someone. Ask the professor how you can improve your learning and grades. Like everyone else, professors like feedback. Occasionally, tell the professor what you liked or had a tough time with in class. This relationship is essential to a better understanding of the content of the course.

Learn What to Write Down

Better to take too many notes than not enough. You can always condense or revise your notes later.

Certainly there is plenty of information you should not write down. But how do you know when something's important? Six common clues tell you when important points are being made by the professor. Pay close attention and take notes when the professor

- tells you something is important.
- repeats a point.
- changes the volume or tone of his voice.
- writes down a point on the chalkboard.
- uses a prop or visual aid.
- tells you it may be on a test.

Figure Out What Motivates You

There are dozens of tools to boost your motivation. In fact, there's a whole section on it later in this book. For the moment, here are a few ways to build your motivation in the class you're taking.

Give yourself a special incentive to learn about the subject. Maybe there's someone else in this class with whom you can study. Find something especially bizarre or interesting about the subject. Collect unusual quotes about the subject, and memorize them for use in a test, a paper, or an essay. Draw a big colorful roadmap of the subject with a **Start Here** arrow. Study what is the toughest part of the subject for you first, instead of last. Study in frequent, short sessions.

Use the Resources Your School Has Available

What can your school offer you? You might be surprised. Some have training in specialized skills available on CD-ROM in the library. Some colleges and universities have counseling offices (if you live in a dorm, it may have such a service, too). Counselors can help with academic (study skills) or personal problems. Find out if tutoring is available. In many cases, it's free or low cost.

Create Extra Accountability

At the college or university level, grades are often posted or mailed. Bring stamped, self-addressed postcards to final exams. Ask the professor to put your grade from the final exam and your final grade for the course on that postcard and mail it to you. This can help you if you're between grades. The professor will be reminded of your interest and may feel a bit more accountable. She may give you the higher grade.

Keep Your Stress Low

Have fun at school. When you need a study break, do something you enjoy. Explore the city or town around your school. Go shopping or out to eat. Take a trip to the mall; take a nap; ride a bike; watch a sunset; walk along the lakefront or beach; reread old letters; make popcorn and watch a favorite movie; call a friend or write a letter; play your favorite sport with friends; read a good novel, magazine, or newspaper.

The Ultimate School Success Tip

You've learned all the strategies, tools, and tips. You have all the confidence, insider secrets, and resources. Now follow these two rules and you'll get top grades:

1. Do just one important thing a day.
2. Then keep doing it.

 When you've read the preceding section, check this box. You're one step closer to your goal!

Review

Once you have finished this, your Day 2 assignment is done. Now, let's review what you accomplished:

✓ You set your goals.
✓ You read the check-in statement.
✓ You understand the importance of beliefs.
✓ You wrote down new, positive beliefs.
✓ You learned three things that boost grades.
✓ You read your review for the day (that's this list).

 Congratulations! You have completed Day 2 of your 30 days. Close the book and we'll see you tomorrow!

Day 3

 Check-in

First, did you complete yesterday's session? If not, hop to it. Then you can start here. This is what's on today's menu:

HOW TO ACCELERATE LEARNING

Accelerated learning is a powerful way to learn. Originated by Dr. G. Lozanov of Bulgaria, this brain-compatible learning works the way your brain naturally loves to learn. In a ten-year nationwide accelerated learning project involving 15,000 students, most raised their grades, some to straight A's! You can do it, too. Just follow the directions in this program. Here are some of the principles.

Surround yourself with positives: positive sayings, affirmations, reminders. Make or buy positive colorful posters for this program. Research suggests that these positive messages work.

Make large colorful mind maps of your material and post them around you where you study. A mind map depicts words and creative symbols concerning all the things you'll study in this class. (See Day 5.) This gives your brain important mental maps for understanding, meaning, and recall.

Use a special kind of music when studying. Studies have shown that certain music is especially good for learning. In addition, other studies have found that listening to Mozart (with headphones preferably) increased thinking skills and intelligence. You might try his Piano Concerto in D Major. More on this kind of music later in this chapter.

Learn to use your mind's special opposite activators. You learn best by alternating active (doing it, role plays, projects) and passive (relaxed visualizing) learning. You learn well by big-picture, global (getting just the highlights) learning alternating with small-points learning (textbook-type details). You learn best by alternating rote (repetition-style) memorization with more episodic and procedural (real life) learning. In general, learning is enhanced by movement, mental movies, rhymes, associations, acting out, sounds, colored pens, large note paper, and picture drawings.

Learn to get into an accelerated learning state of mind. You have had times in your life when you were totally focused, determined to succeed, no matter what. In your imagination, take yourself back to one of those times. Now bring that confident state of mind to the present. Use it for optimal studying and to accomplish terrific results in the least possible time.

   When you've read the preceding section, check this box. You're one step closer to your goal!

SET UP THE OPTIMAL STUDY ENVIRONMENT

We never work, think, or play in a vacuum. There is always a certain context—a location and specific circumstances. These have a direct biological, sociological, and psychological impact on you and your studying. As you set up your learning environment, whether in a dorm, apartment, sorority or fraternity house, give yourself every chance you can to succeed.

Use Proper Lighting

How much does the lighting matter? Research suggests that it matters a great deal. Dr. Wayne London's 1988 experiments caught worldwide attention. London, a Vermont psychiatrist, switched the lighting in three elementary school classrooms halfway through the school year from fluorescent lighting to Vitalite full-spectrum lighting.

The results were amazing. London found that the students who were in the classrooms with full-spectrum lighting missed fewer school days than those in the other classrooms. London said, "Ordinary fluorescent light has been shown to raise the cortisol level in the blood, a change likely to suppress the immune system." This affects other areas in learning.

Dr. D.B. Harmon studied 160,000 school-age children to determine which, if any, environmental factors influenced their learning. The results of his research were amazing. By the time they graduated from elementary school (age 11–12), over 50 percent of the student subjects had developed deficiencies related to classroom lighting!

To test the hypothesis, changes were made in the students' learning environment, and the same children were studied six months later. The results of the change were equally dramatic: visual problems reduced 65 percent, fatigue reduced 55 percent, infections decreased

43 percent, and posture problems dropped 25 percent. In addition, those same students showed a dramatic increase in academic achievement.

Current research suggests that the best lighting for reading is low to moderate levels of natural lighting. The second best choice is full-spectrum fluorescent or incandescent lighting. Indirect lighting is best since it keeps eye fatigue lowest. Do what you can to provide the best lighting for yourself. You may be surprised how something so simple can return such big rewards.

Cool Temperature

How much does temperature affect your reading? Dr. Robert Ornstein reports that the brain is far more efficient with a three-degree temperature decrease than a three-degree temperature increase. In U.S. Defense Department studies, Taylor and Orlansky report that heat stress dramatically lowers scores in both intellectual and physical tasks. High temperatures were responsible for decreases in performance requiring accuracy, speed, dexterity, and physical acuity. While many types of obstacles and barriers are known to reduce or impair learning, heat stress is one of the most preventable. Keep your studying environment cool (not cold) for best attention, focus, and comprehension. For most learners, this means in the 65–70 degree range.

Pleasant Surroundings

Our brains make connections and associations with almost everything—some of them good, others not so good. We connect feelings to people, places, objects, and events. A photograph, a chair, a face, a song, an activity or even a plant can bring back a specific memory or release a whole flood of positive or negative memories. It makes sense to do everything in your power to have more positive than negative associations with what you'll be seeing in your studying environment.

Scientists at the National Aeronautics and Space Administration have discovered that the use of plants creates a better scientific, learning, and thinking environment for astronauts. Could their same research apply to learners indoors? Dr. Wolverton, who headed the Environmental Research Laboratory, says that some plants have improved life for the astronauts as well as his own personal life at home. He says that they remove pollutants from the air, increase the negative ionization, and charge it with oxygen. In fact, according to the Federal Clean Air Council, studies discovered that plants raised the oxygen levels and increased productivity by 10 percent. Additionally, the ideal atmosphere is between 60–80 percent humidity.

In addition, minimize distractions (both visual or auditory) when you study so that you will not be disturbed. You might unplug your phone or put on an answering machine. You might do your reading in a place that allows you to concentrate or place a "Do Not Disturb" sign on the door. Does your specific study location matter? Only to the degree that you will or won't do well in it. Find a good location and stick to it.

The Use of Specific Aromas

While you can tune out certain sounds like traffic, an air conditioner, or passersby, smells are different. They are processed directly by the mid-brain area (hypothalamus). This means we get the full impact of aromas before we've had a chance to even think about them. Years of research have been done on the impact of aromas on thinking and learning. Aromatherapists have specifically identified certain scents influential in mental alertness and in relaxation.

Mental alertness	Relaxation
Lemon	Lavender
Cinnamon	Orange
Peppermint	Rose
Basil	Chamomile

It turns out that several specific scents can positively stimulate our attention and memory. Two of the best are lemon and peppermint. How do you get those into your environment? Several ways. You can cut up a fresh lemon and leave it out nearby. You can buy lemon or peppermint oils and put them on a fan, heater, or candle. You can also brew herbal teas or use room fresheners that have those aromas. While the processed effects are not for everyone, you might be pleasantly surprised how well they work for you.

Appropriate Music

Can listening to music help learning, studying, or even raise intelligence? One study measured the impact of listening to music before taking a standardized test. It was conducted by researcher Dr. Gordon Shaw at the University of California at Irvine. The students who listened for ten minutes (Mozart's Sonata for Two Pianos in D Major) raised their test scores in spatial and abstract reasoning. On an intelligence test, the gain was nine points after just ten minutes! Although the effect on the brain is only temporary, the results can be duplicated with additional reactivation at any time. Those who listened only to a relaxation tape or had silence either improved only slightly or stayed the same. Researchers agree that more studies are needed to discover the effects of other music and timing on intelligence scores.

A 1987 National Music Educators Conference report says students taking music courses scored 20–40 points higher on standardized college entrance exams. A college entrance examination board study discovered that students who took four or more years of music classes scored higher on both verbal and

MU – SIC WILL STIM-U – LATE YOUR MIND

math tests. Of the countries with the top-rated science and math results, all of them have strong music and art programs.

How does music do this? It activates more than the right brain. It elicits emotional responses, receptive or aggressive states, and stimulates the limbic system. The limbic system and subcortical region are involved in engaging musical and emotional responses. More importantly, research has documented the role of the hippocampus in long-term memory. When information is imbued with music, there's a greater likelihood that the brain will encode it in long-term memory.

Research suggests that many learners understand and recall better when music is being played. The percentage of learners who fall into this type of category varies dramatically. You would get a different response from musicians than from more visual learners. Learner preference for some low volume background music (such as Baroque, in a major key) runs from a low of 20 percent to a high of 75–80 percent. You might try Vivaldi's *Four Seasons*, Handel's *Water Music* or even some environmental sounds. Waterfalls or ocean waves can be productive. For best results, experiment.

Proper Reading Posture

How you sit affects how you feel. This in turn affects your attitude about what you read as well as how you read it. The best posture for reading is sitting upright with your back straight or bent slightly forward. Lying down, lounging, or slouching impair alertness and concentration. Sit at a table, resting the book at about a 45-

degree angle from the table. This gives your eyes a clear, full view of the whole page. This decreases eye strain considerably. You might place a two to three-inch-thick book or notebook under the book you are reading to decrease neck strain from looking down.

Most of the time readers place books too close to the eyes. If you have good vision, corrected or not, you might find less eye strain by placing a book a few inches further away.

Negatively Charged Air

All air, inside or outside, has an electrical charge. These charged particles are called ions. It seems that when it comes to air, the more negatively charged it is, the better. Smoke, dust, smog, pollutants, electrical emissions, heating and cooling systems, and traffic are all detrimental culprits. With these, the air becomes more highly electrified (too many positive ions) and humans react. Studies suggest between 57–85 percent of the population is strongly affected and can improve dramatically with more negative ions.

The impact of negatively charged air on the body is powerful. Originally, it was found to speed recovery in burn or asthma patients. It was later discovered to affect serotonin levels in the bloodstream, to stabilize alpha rhythms, and to positively impact our reactions to sensory stimuli. Ornstein reports that rats exposed to negative ionization grew a 9 percent larger cerebral cortex. In other words, the electrical charge in the air boosted brain size! The greater levels of alertness can translate into improved learning.

Dr. Kornblueh of the American Institute of Medical Climatology was among the first to demonstrate the dramatic effect that the electrical charge in the air has on our behavior. His work at Pennsylvania Graduate Hospital and Frankford Hospital in Philadelphia led him to make negative ionization a permanent part of hospital treatments. Many corporations, including ABC, Westinghouse, General Electric, Carrier, Philco, and Emerson now use ion generators in the workplace. What can you do to increase the negative ionization of the air you breathe? Several things can help: 1) increase the amount of live plants; 2) get fresh outside air in your environment; 3) sit near indoor aquariums, waterfalls, or humidifiers; 4) purchase an ionizer (call [800] 382-IONS for a small one (room size).

Mobility

Many learners feel compelled to stay seated to learn. It's almost as if the ghost of a professor is lurching over them. But, it turns out, you may actually learn better by moving around often. You might want to get up and walk around while you think things through. You might want to sit in a way that you can tap your feet or rock your chair. Mobility, even simply standing up, can boost learning.

Dr. Max Vercruyssen of the University of Southern California discovered your body's posture affects learning. His research showed that, on the average, standing increased heartbeats by ten extra beats per minute. That sends more blood to the brain, which activates the central nervous system to increase neural firing.

Researchers found that on the average there's a 5–15 percent greater flow of blood and oxygen to the brain when standing. Could you place a book on a counter top and, while standing, read for a couple of minutes? You may be surprised at how well it works. Before you decide one way or another, give it a try.

Hydration

Dr. Hannaford, in her book *Smart Moves*, asserts that the average learner is often dehydrated. This dehydration leads to poor learning performance. Your brain works on a complex electrolyte formula that requires the ideal balance, just like a car battery. Too much or too little sodium or potassium can be disastrous to your brain. Fortunately, those are well regulated by your own automatic mechanisms. Water, however is another story.

Learning specialists recommend from 8 to 12 glasses per day, depending on your body size, the weather, and your activity level. Nutritionists recommend pure water to ensure that it is free of contaminants. It's also better to have pure water rather than soft drinks, coffee, or tea. They act as diuretics and your body needs even more water to make up the deficit. Professors have found that in classrooms where students are encouraged to drink water as often as needed, behavior improves, as does performance. Cut down the amount of soft drinks, tea, or coffee. Start replacing them with glasses of water. You'll be pleased with the difference.

Breaks

The brain is very poor at maintaining a continuous, sustained focus. It's better at short bursts. Sometimes your reading bursts might be ten minutes, other times as long as 30 to 50 minutes, but rarely longer than that. Feel free to take breaks. They are normal and natural ways that the brain rides out the effects of nutrition, hormones, and environmental stimuli.

Many students have found an egg timer, a stopwatch, or a digital watch with an alarm useful in keeping a tight schedule. Others let their bodies' own natural rhythms tell them when it's time. Experiment and you'll find out which is best for you.

What do you think? Are your reading/studying conditions optimal? While study environment is not the only thing that makes the difference between a poor and excellent student, it's one thing that you have some control of. And you can change it right now. Before you go any further, do what you can to set up your ideal studying environment. List three things you can do:

1. _Play Classical Music_
2. _Light a lemon/peppermint Candle_
3. _Study where there aren't any distractions._

☑ When you've read the preceding section, check this box. You're one step closer to your goal!

Review

Once you have finished this, your Day 3 assignment is done. Not bad! Before you go do something else, let's review what you accomplished:

✓ You made the decision to read this chapter.
✓ You read the check-in statement.
✓ You learned tips on how to accelerate learning.
✓ You learned how to make the optimal studying environment.
✓ You read your review for the day (that's this list).

 Congratulations! You have completed Day 3 of your 30 days. Close the book and we'll see you tomorrow!

Day 4

 Check-in
First, did you finish yesterday's chapter? If not, do it now. Then you can start today's action.

STUDY SKILLS THAT WORK

Your new study process consists of a simple, street-smart set of strategies designed to make your learning come alive. It is based on the multilayered learning process and actually takes less time than your old method of study. It may seem longer at first, but each step takes less time, and because it is so well structured, you will have better success at test time. Here we go—the following is your surefire study process.

1. Prestudy
   ♦ Set purpose and goals.
   ♦ Copy chapter titles.
   ♦ Structure notes.

2. Ask yourself key questions
   ♦ Turn every title and subtitle into a question.
   ♦ Add subtitles and main ideas to notes.
   ♦ Add key ideas to your notes and maps.

3. Gather what you need
   ♦ Read to answer questions.

- Stay active, write, think, pause.
- Use a pencil check system; make notes, under-line.
- Add details to notes for each page.

4. Evaluate and correct

- Find out what you know and don't know.
- Fill gaps in notes where needed.
- Answer questions.
- Make what you've learned meaningful in personal terms.
- Move from short-term to long-term memory.

Time and again students have proved that a multi-layered study process is much more effective than spending all your time reading and highlighting. The only way to learn the material is to become actively involved in absorbing and integrating it. Studying is an active process, not a passive one. So get pumped up—you're ready to learn!

Get Your Mind Ready

How do you prepare your mind? Start with these simple suggestions. Get rid of distractions. Do your best to reduce the amounts of paper on your desk, distracting pictures, or other clutter. Keep the music low or off. Make sure the phone is unable to bother you and put a Quiet sign on your door. Go somewhere to read or study that puts you in a good, upright, active learning posture. Maybe the library? Put a glass of water on your desk and wear loose clothes.

Get rid of any distracting thoughts by writing them down to deal with later. Make sure your room is at the right temperature, cool (not cold) with good air circulation and good lighting. Next, get out your study materials and organize them. Figure out what you have, what you're missing. Get out your assignment. Take a big deep breath and relax. Finally, you're ready to go. Next, start browsing.

Why browse? Browsing primes your mind for learning. The brain is poorly designed for digesting new big ideas or concepts. But it is very good at nibbling at ideas that become big ideas. Browsing provides the mind with hooks through preexposure to a topic. It is almost as if it gives your brain little mental Post-its with which to emphasize information later on.

What to browse? Browse the resources you need for your classes and assignments. These resources include, but are not limited to:

1. CD-ROM files
2. textbooks
3. the Internet
4. library books
5. videos
6. museums
7. your dorm, apartment, or home
8. magazines, journals, newsletters
9. class notes

How do you browse? The process of browsing is simple.

1. Locate your source.
2. Take no more than five to 30 seconds per page to glance over it.
3. Note all headlines, subtitles, and graphics.
4. Find out if this source has what you want.
5. Make a mental note of what is located where, so you can go back later to dig into it.

For example, in a textbook, you'll want to get an overview. Start by turning pages quickly to scan the information. Gather short answers to the following questions.

1. What are the main topics?
2. What do I already know about these topics?
3. What special terminology is used to present the topics?
4. Who is the author?
5. How is the book organized?
6. How difficult is the material?

Create a Mental Map

Have you ever tried (or would you even dare) to put together a jigsaw puzzle without knowing the picture on the outside of the puzzle box? It would be nearly hopeless! Your brain learns very poorly with isolated fragments of information. But it learns very well with knowing the big picture. When you're studying, how can you visualize the equivalent of the picture on the puzzle box? It's simple. You take a few moments and draw the pieces. Do you need to be an artist? No. If you've got paper, pencil, and any ideas at all, you can create a mental map of the material.

Begin to structure your thinking like the structure of the book you're reading. Decide how much material you wish to learn. Draw a picture of the organization of it. You can use fish-bone diagrams (think of what a skeleton of a common fish looks like) or other visual/graphic techniques. You might experiment a bit: put the more important information to the left, details to the right. Use fewer words and more colored pens. Leave more room under topics and titles that have more pages involved. Draw these maps and lines before reading to help your mind organize and store the data better. After a chapter or section, go back and add to your notes. You might find the table of contents and do searches for key words. You might stop on the more interesting parts and give them a closer look. Make a mental note of what's available and where it's located. Once you've finished this initial step, the browsing part is done.

Ask Questions

The browsing process does many important things for your education—especially in planting the seed for learning. But now it's time to start to get your brain in high gear. Since the mind works very well at finding answers to questions, let's start with asking questions first. The more questions you ask, the more ways you prime your mind to find answers. You've already browsed the material, so you know what's easy, what's hard. You already know where the meat of it is and where the fluff is. Now, let's start with the real learning.

Go on a hunt for questions in your material. Move quickly, skimming through the chapters much faster than your reading rate. Your purpose here is to find out what is important and how it is presented, not to read it.

You'll have two categories of questions. The *first group* helps you stand back and identify what you need and want from the material. Here are examples of such questions, which can and should form part of your pre-reading habit.

➤ What is my final application of this reading material?

➤ How important is this material to me?

➤ What are the professor's expectations?

➤ Do I want to recall specific facts and details?

The *second group* of questions you'll ask are more content related. In order to be able to ask powerful pre-reading questions, you'll want to scan the material very quickly first. Check all boldface headings, turning each into a question you will answer later. Here are some examples:

Heading/Chapter Subtitle:
Computer Software Piracy

Your possible questions:
"Legally, what is computer piracy?"
"How does it work?"
"Where and who?"

Key words are critical. During this step, go quickly through the material to locate anything that prompts your brain for a question. The possibilities include

- anything with bullets.
- anything with titles.
- all the subtitles.
- table of contents.
- headings.
- subheadings.
- front and back covers.
- first and last pages of books.
- copyright date.
- index.
- text in boldface or italic.
- first and last paragraphs of any sections.
- sections and material in boxes.
- any figures or charts.
- chapter summaries.
- previews or review questions.
- anything that catches your attention.

You might say, "But I need answers, not just a bunch of questions." However, at this stage of your progress with the material, the questions will do more for you, in the long run, than any answers. Questions will give your brain a goal, so it can go into search-and-find mode. Questions keep being processed on many levels long after you've found an answer. Questions stimulate thinking, answers don't.

At times, you will literally find everything you want to know just through this scanning process. That's one of the unexpected joys of prereading. You'll learn what to expect, where to look for important information. In time, this step will become the most valued part of your overall reading process.

Creating a Study Strategy and Goals

The whole point of prereading is to gain enough information to decide on a strategy for studying the material. If you go through all the time and work to pre-read and do nothing with the information, it was a waste.

Now is the time in the prereading process for you to make a specific time commitment. Now is the time for you to adjust your strategies. Do you read all or part of the material? Do you take notes or not? No longer are you an open-to-the-first-page-and-go type of student. You're savvy and sharp.

Look over the visual aids, such as maps, charts, diagrams, illustrations, and pictures. This will help you grasp each point quickly. Then read any summaries or questions included at the end of the chapter. Summaries are helpful because they include the points the author felt to be most important.

Now, before proceeding with your study, set two goals. Set a *comprehension goal*—decide how well you need to know the material. Will you be tested? If so, how thoroughly? Set a *time goal* for your particular section or chapter based upon how well you need to know it. With easy or familiar material, your goal may be 15 pages an hour. Whatever your goal, make sure that it is only for one chapter or section—setting lengthy or unrealistic goals only leads to discouragement and failure. By achieving both of these goals, you will speed your study time greatly.

Gathering Answers

So far, you've made two passes at the material. It took some time, but it was well worth it. You figured out the overall pattern to your material, then you primed your mind for gathering the rich information and meaning you want. In short, you've gotten yourself ready to read fast and with high comprehension. In fact, if you already think you have a feel for the material, great! That's exactly what you want to have. If you still feel foggy about the material, that's fine, too. You're about to get a good opportunity to make some real progress in the comprehension department.

Now it's time to get focused, to get the answers to the questions you've been posing. Read the chapter as quickly as you can to understand the ideas. After each page or major idea, go back to your notes and add the supporting details to them. Go no more than a page without writing something down. This is an important key to textbook comprehension and retention. Respond to the material by continually summarizing it in your notes, using your own words.

The old way of studying was to read and forget. Get into the habit of reading and responding. You will find even the most boring books become interesting. Avoid marking the text with highlighters at this point. It's too early to judge what is most important until you've read the entire chapter. It also postpones learning and you might just end up with an expensive coloring book! Coloring is not learning.

Whenever something looks valuable, pencil a check mark in the margin, just to the side of the passage. It marks what is important, but is not permanent. Later on, during a review, you can reevaluate your marks and either leave them in place, erase them, or add a second one for emphasis. This system is one of the most valuable tools you can use. Not only is it flexible, but it is quite inexpensive. Continue reading each chapter, or section, marking what is important with a check, and adding to your notes until you are finished.

Evaluate and Respond

Are you still with us? Hang in there, we have just a bit more to go. Your mind is learning to acquire information in a far better way than the old way of stare and hope. This is a much more active process and it takes time and energy. But the rewards are well worth it. Let's figure out what we have and what we don't. Use this as a quick mental checklist:

➤ Go back to the beginning of your material and browse it quickly to refresh your memory.

➤ Answer the chapter questions provided by the author.

➤ Answer your own questions.

➤ What are the key relationships?

➤ Can you talk about each chapter title, topic, and subtopic you studied from the table of contents?

➤ Do you now have mental details to support each main idea?

➤ Can you study that chapter from your notes?

When you get used to knowing those types of questions and answers, you'll be a successful learner. Why? Part of succeeding at learning is to know what you don't know and to know what questions to ask. Your goal so far has been to get the key meaning, the key concepts, the key material out of the text into your notes (via your mind).

Practice recalling information with and without your notes. Learn to study and reflect as much as possible from your notes. They are bound to be more understandable than the text. Avoid rereading your texts over and over. Browse them from now on and use them only when searching for an answer to a specific question.

From Short-Term to Long-Term Memory

There are many ways that you can transfer learning from short-term to long-term memory. The single most critical ingredient is to process the learning—do something with it. It's a poor use of your time to read something and forget it. You're too busy and the stakes are too high. If it's worth learning, make it worth recalling. There's a whole chapter coming up on tips to embed learning in long-term memory. But here are just a few specific tips.

➤ Summarize the knowledge on paper in your notes.

➤ Review the material in different environments.

➤ Implement and really use the knowledge in your personal life.

➤ Make a simple video or audiotape about the material.

➤ Transfer notes to your computer and use them.

➤ Use the concept of mnemonics/acronym to remember facts.

➤ Create or redo a song or make a rap about what you've learned.

➤ Make up and tell a story about it.

➤ Attach a strong emotion to it.

➤ Repeat and review it within ten minutes, 48 hours, and seven days.

➤ Make a concrete reminder: a token or artifact, like a political button, about it.

➤ Act it out or do a fun role play about it.

➤ Put it on a picture or poster—use intense colors.

➤ Use a real situation as practice for learning it, if possible.

➤ Hold unguided discussion on the material with a peer.

➤ Follow the learning up with journal writing.

➤ Build a working model of what you learned.

➤ Find a buddy/support group.

➤ Divide the material into smaller, more manageable chunks of information—but no more than three or four chunks at a time.

The use of these tools, which we'll explore in more detail in later chapters, will be one of your most worthwhile investments. Remember, it's not what you know, it's if you know it in the right context when you really need it. Most likely your exams are a test of your thinking, writing, and recalling abilities, not just your reading skills. So practice thinking, practice writing, and practice recalling your notes and the text material. The study process you have just learned demands proof of your effectiveness through organization and recall. It is simple, yet effective. Let's review the four parts.

1. Prestudy
2. Ask yourself key questions

3. Gather what you need
4. Evaluate and correct

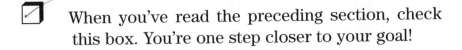 When you've read the preceding section, check this box. You're one step closer to your goal!

LEARN THE POWER OF HABITS

There's a single overriding thought you can take from this book. The way you are, from now on, is up to you. You can shape your destiny. You can choose what kind of future you will have. You can form the habits that will literally guide you to success. If this reminder that *you* determine your success seems corny, think again. Every year thousands of students decide to take a new path and learn to get better grades. Some do it in a course or seminar, others from a tutor, professor, parent, friend, or book.

It takes courage to try out and keep new habits. You can either choose the habits of success or the habits of fear. The habits of success are the ones outlined in this book. The path of fear is to avoid doing the daily chapters. Why? Some students fear that they can't do it. So they figure "Better to not try and to fail, than to try and fail. At least no one will know." Others are afraid they will succeed. That means they will have to change their low self-esteem or confidence. It means their friends will think of them differently, and so will their parents and professors.

It's time to make a decision. Do you want to become good at these success skills once and for all? If so, here are three suggestions for you.

Start Now

To make the transition from bad study habits to using these success skills, it's best to go cold turkey. Just jump in and make it happen. You can start at any time, in any class, with any skill level. Avoid waiting until you have perfected these skills. They'll always be in the process of getting better.

DIVE IN

Think Positively

Give up any negative thoughts or inner voices about being a poor student. One student said, "I just don't think I am cut out to learn this. And if I did learn it, I wouldn't learn it well. And if I get it, I won't enjoy it. And if I enjoy it, my skills won't last." That's an example of a pattern that will cause failure.

Here's a different attitude. Another student said, "I am going to learn this one way or another. If I get stuck,

I'll find another way. If I don't do well, I'll reread the book and find out where I went wrong. If my skills are weak, I'll practice more. In fact, I'll do whatever it takes to master this."

Imagine the Habit

Now is the time to begin to master the power of habits. Practice makes permanent. Every thought you think makes the likelihood of thinking that thought again even higher. Be careful what you say, what you think or dream—that affects your future! Begin the practice in your mind. Read this section over first, then go back and do the exercises.

Close your eyes. Take a moment to paint a vivid mental picture of the kind of learning you encounter regularly. Visualize yourself improving the concentration, comprehension, and retention of what you study. You complete your studying with ease. You are relaxed and calm. You know you can recall the information any time you'd like. You look at your clear desk feeling ready for the following day. You know you can now succeed at courses to complete degrees, gain promotions, learn new skills, expand your knowledge, and satisfy your general curiosity. You glance at course outlines knowing you can stay ahead of the required reading and perform with excellence.

Make your habits easy. One college student kept misplacing his car keys. Why? There was no habit of putting them in the same place. He decided to put a special hook just inside the desk in his dorm room. Now, every time he wants to leave, he reaches for that hook and the keys are always there. He has made it a habit to put his keys on the hook every single time.

What habits do you wish you had? A habit to study every night? Make it easy to study! Put out a reminder sign for yourself: STUDY TIME 8–10 P.M. NIGHTLY. Tell others to leave you alone during that time. Start getting ready to study at 7:50, not 8 P.M.

Do something once, it's an action. Do it several times and a habit beings to form. The sum of your habits is your character. The quality of your character is the quality of your life. Habits are powerful.

Review

Once you have finished this, your day's assignment is done. While it's fresh, let's review what you accomplished:

✓ You made the decision to continue this program.
✓ You found the best system to prepare for reading.
✓ You learned the importance of asking questions.
✓ You learned how to gather answers.
✓ You found out how to evaluate and respond.
✓ You learned about the power of habits.
✓ You read your review for the day (that's this list).

 Congratulations! You have completed Day 4 of your 30 days. Close the book and we'll see you tomorrow!

Day 5

 Check-in
First, are you finished with yesterday's chapter?
If not, do it now.

SUPER NOTE TAKING

You learn in many ways: by seeing, by doing, by writing, and by listening. Professors expect you to do most of your learning by listening, then taking notes. The super note-taking system described here will help make the job easier:

♦ Its flexibility allows for those times when the professor drops one idea and starts up another.

♦ It uses both the left side of the brain, which processes words, and the right side of the brain, which processes colors, relationships, pictures, and symbols.

♦ It helps you remember your notes later on.

♦ It is fun to use.

The system is called visual mapping. Fast replacing traditional note-taking methods in schools across the nation, it's easy to learn and works so well that you can expect to recall from 80 to 100 percent of your notes.

A visual map is a creative pattern of connected ideas. It is similar to a sentence diagram, a road map, or a blueprint. Although it is often called clustering or grouping,

NOTE TAKING BY MAPPING

there are some important differences that you'll soon
discover. The steps are easy.

1. **Start with a topic and enclose it in the center
   of your paper** with a circle or other symbol. This
   gives your mind a central focus and reminds you
   constantly of the key idea. Use about 10 percent of
   the paper for the title—about the size of an egg.
2. **Add branches for key ideas or subtopics.** You
   might get these key ideas from the professor's
   lesson or from boldface print and chapter subtitles in your textbook. Or you might create likely categories such as who, what, where, why, and
   how.

   You might like to add the branches going
   around the visual map in a circle, like spokes on
   a wheel. Go ahead and start at about the ten
   o'clock position for the first branch. Then add

each remaining branch in a pattern. You might add the next at one o'clock and then at four o'clock. This keeps your notes in order.

On larger topics, branches might represent a segment (such as history, geography, or sociology) or be ordered chronologically. In fiction, branches could be labeled for character, setting, plot, conflicts, and resolution.

3. **Add details to the branches.** Each subtopic will have more details or key words that can be added. In general, the fewer the better, but you'll usually have three to eight words per branch.

4. **Personalize it for the right (not left) brain.** The secret to making visual mapping work is to add pictures, symbols, cartoons, illustrations, and drawings. Here are some tips on how to personalize it.

 ◆ Use your paper horizontally.

 ◆ Use medium-thick felt-tip pens in at least three colors.

 ◆ Use pictures and symbols for every key idea. Any symbol will work, as long as it makes sense to you.

 ◆ Print all words on lines, using upper and lowercase. Vary the size of words by level of importance. Do not write words upside down; keep all words near the middle of the page and easy to read.

 ◆ Use a different color for each branch, and use arrows to show relationships.

 ◆ Put cReAtiViTy, **zest,** *action* and ***personality*** into it.

To see how easy, fun, and effective visual mapping can be, make a map with you as the topic. Put your name in the center. Then make branches for each of the areas in your life, such as family, parties, school, health and fitness, hobbies, and best friends. Now fill out your visual map. If you run out of room, make two visual maps! Examples are given throughout this section. These are only a few of many possible styles and kinds of visual maps. Visual mapping for English class? No problem. Visual maps for history? No problem. Visual maps for math? No problem. Page 52 is a visual map of a whole book. The title's in the center.

Visual maps have many uses—studying, generating ideas, personal note taking, planning, reviewing, problem solving, writing speeches. There are plenty of others—use your imagination!

MASTER SELF-TALK FOR MORE CONFIDENCE

Self-talk is what you say to yourself. You say, "I don't do that!" Guess what—just did! What you say to yourself can determine your mood. It's also one of the ways you control your brain. What you say to yourself is much more important than what others say to you. You can't always control what others say to you, but you *can* control what you say to yourself.

What you say to yourself influences both your feelings and your actions. It affects what you think and how you feel about yourself—your self-image, self-concept, self-esteem, and self-worth. You are what you think of

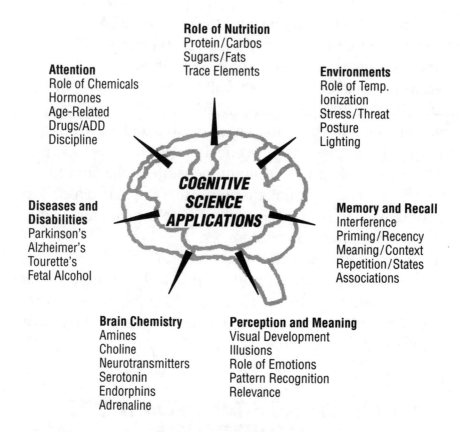

Role of Nutrition
Protein/Carbos
Sugars/Fats
Trace Elements

Attention
Role of Chemicals
Hormones
Age-Related
Drugs/ADD
Discipline

Environments
Role of Temp.
Ionization
Stress/Threat
Posture
Lighting

COGNITIVE SCIENCE APPLICATIONS

Diseases and Disabilities
Parkinson's
Alzheimer's
Tourette's
Fetal Alcohol

Memory and Recall
Interference
Priming/Recency
Meaning/Context
Repetition/States
Associations

Brain Chemistry
Amines
Choline
Neurotransmitters
Serotonin
Endorphins
Adrenaline

Perception and Meaning
Visual Development
Illusions
Role of Emotions
Pattern Recognition
Relevance

yourself. If you value your time highly, others usually will, too. If you think you're a second-rate student, others often treat you that way. And if you think you should be an A student, professors will be more willing to help you achieve that reality.

Self-talk can also make you feel negative, so you don't want to do things you really ought to do. Examples of negative self-talk: "Studying is hard; I can't do it." "I don't know how to do this." "I'm lost." "This doesn't make sense to me." Whenever you say those words, you give them a kind of power or control over your life. For the same effort, you might as well use positive words instead of negative ones.

First Easy Step

1. First, learn to catch yourself saying negative things, such as "I can't" and "There's no way" or "I don't know how."
2. Then, learn to add a simple magic word or phrase to the end of it, so you think positively. Every time you say "I can't," add the words, "so far" or "yet." Learn to say "I don't know how to do this YET." Learn to say "I can't do this SO FAR." Learn to say, "This doesn't make sense to me YET."

The phrase, "There's no way," can be altered in many ways. For example, "I don't know a way to do this, but I'll find a way."

If you can start adding such positive words every time you think a negative thought, it will make a difference. It simply takes a bit of time for it to become a habit. How about beginning today? Are you willing to give it a try?

☑ If you are, check this box.

Review

Once you have finished this, your assignment is done. Before you move on to something else, let's review what you accomplished.

✓ You made the decision to continue the program.
✓ You read about better ways to take notes.
✓ You saw examples of notes to stir your imagination.
✓ You discovered the power of self-talk.
✓ You promised to begin making your self-talk more positive.
✓ You read your review for the day (that's this list).

 Congratulations! You have completed Day 5 of your 30 days. Close the book and we'll see you tomorrow!

Day 6

 Check-in

Are you finished with yesterday's chapter?
Cool! Your first week is shaping up. Today will be an easy day.

TOTAL RECALL

Today, we'll do a photoflash sneak preview of the whole book. You've done this before, on Day 1. It's so beneficial, we'll do it again several more times. It gives your brain sneak previews well in advance. It plants seeds for future learning and makes each day have more meaning when you do get to it. And instead of trying to recall everything you've learned, every single day, we'll do simple weekly reviews.

PHOTOFLASH

You will be able to do it easily. Here's a quick pre-view. You simply take a look at each page for the short-est length of time you can (like a photoflash). Let your brain absorb as much or as a little as naturally happens in that time. Merely glance at the page for one second or less, then look at the next page. Use a relaxed, soft focus with your eyes, purposely *not* trying to read any-thing. Just glance at it like you would a picture. At one second per page, this entire book (all 30 chapters) will go very quickly.

You'll continue doing this toward the end of each seven-day cycle. By the end of the course, this same exercise becomes a powerful review. And it will take very little time, too. Go ahead and photoflash every page in this book. That's all you do today. Turn pages and glance at them.

   When you're done, check this box.

Review

You're through with today's assignment. Before you move ahead, let's review what you accomplished.

✓ You made the decision to continue the program.
✓ You read the check-in statement.
✓ You photoflashed the whole 30-day program.
✓ You read your review for the day (that's this list).

   Congratulations! You have completed Day 6 of your 30 days. Close the book and we'll see you tomorrow!

Day 7

FREE DAY

Today is a free day. It means you can do whatever your heart desires. Visit friends, play a sport, practice an instrument, see a movie, work out, watch TV, or work on a project. You can also spend important time doing something you've been putting off for a while. Yes, you can study if you are behind and have to catch up on a class or assignment, but make sure you get some down time. Go to it!

Review

Once you have finished this, today's assignment is complete. Before you close the book and move on to something else, let's review what you accomplished.

✓ You made the decision to continue the program.
✓ You read the check-in statement.
✓ You figured out what you want to do for fun today.
✓ You read your review for the day (that's this list).

 Congratulations! You have completed Day 7 of your 30 days. Your first week is done; that's 25 percent! Close the book and relax.

Day 8

 Check-in

Are you ready for today? If you are, start here. Today we'll learn some awesome skills, such as how to read F-A-S-T!

SPEED READING, PART I

Reading requires both attitude and skill. The whole purpose of reading is to comprehend it, which means to understand it. You can have good comprehension reading slowly or quickly. You might as well have it reading quickly! And here's the good news: you *can* improve your speed and your comprehension at the same time.

Speed Reading Is Another World

Before you begin to speed read, you might have a few questions: How different is speed reading from regular reading? Will I miss out on things? Will I speed read everything? Once you understand the answers to these questions, you'll be on a better footing for reading fast.

Let's use some examples for starters. First, the difference between traveling by foot and by bicycle is not just a change in speed. The difference between a bicycle and a car is more than just going faster. And certainly the difference between traveling by airplane and traveling by automobile is greater than saving a few hours.

These examples are important to understand because passenger jets did more than help us get to the other side of the country. They changed the way we think about distances. They changed how we feel about relationships, business, culture, friendships, geography, and the world. And now, the Internet and the World Wide Web are doing the same.

Speed reading opens up new possibilities in your life. It will change your relationships with information. It changes how you think about your goals, your potential, and yourself. It makes the impossible seem possible. It frees up your time for other things. It allows you to become an expert in much less time.

In short, it has the capacity to change your life. If you want everything to stay the same in your life, speed reading may not be for you. However, if you'd like to enter a whole new world of possibilities, it may become one of the most exciting things you've ever done for yourself. Before you start, here's a few other questions you may want answered.

Does speed reading require more intelligence? No it doesn't. It does require better preparation and concentration. You can develop those two. But as long as you can read, you can read faster. It requires skill, will, and practice. You'll learn to concentrate better and read for shorter lengths of time.

Will I speed read everything? No. But you'll have a wider range of reading rates than before. For example, you'll read poetry, love letters, and directions as slowly as ever. But after learning speed reading, you'll be reading textbooks and other things much faster.

How will I remember it all? It will take more practice in recalling. Before, in five minutes, you might have read one page or three pages. Soon, you'll be reading five, ten, or 20 pages in a minute's time. That's a whole new scale of speed; daydream and you'll miss a page. In addition, over a given hour, you'll have far more data to store and recall.

What will be different in my life? Many things. It will change how you think of books. You'll no longer pick a book by its thickness. You'll gain self-confidence. You may find yourself setting higher goals for yourself. Most of all, you're likely to realize that the whole world is now at your fingertips. You could become an expert in a subject in six months!

How long will it take to learn it? You're likely to see and feel progress within a week. With a commitment of five or ten minutes of practice a day, you'll be a strong, fast, confident reader in just 30 days.

What will be the key changes in my actual reading? The first one will be that you'll learn reading for meaning, not for words. This will enable you to take in larger chunks of information. The second one is that some of your reading will become far more active. You'll be more strategic and purposeful about how you read and what you read.

Will it still feel like my old way of reading? No. The only thing that will feel like your old way of reading is your old way of reading. Walking feels different than sitting. Riding a bicycle feels different than riding in a car—you see, hear, and feel a whole new set of sensations. It will be different. They cannot and should not be compared. Each has its own advantages. For one, it'll take time more often to review what you've learned.

What principles actually allow me to read faster? Many things. First, the use of your natural peripheral vision, since that lets you see wider areas of print. Second, your new and different strategies for approaching reading will help. Third, a fresh attitude about the realistic possibilities of reading faster. Finally, the eye and mind practice will help seal the deal.

How long will my speed reading last? It's a group of skills. The skills will last as long as you use them. Use them each week, at least several times, and you'll have them for years.

What's my biggest challenge? The fact that it's not common yet. Sometimes you'll feel funny reading fast in public, but that will give way, over time, to confidence. After all, some others who are either insecure or jealous may needle you and give you a hard time.

HOW TO START SPEED READING

These are the five keys to becoming a great speed reader.

- mental practice
- peripheral practice

- vertical practice
- speed practice
- comprehension practice

Practice Makes Permanent

The old expression practice makes perfect has a built-in assumption: that you are practicing correctly. In reality, what you practice is more likely to become permanent than to become perfect.

The design of your brain is such that every thought you think creates a neural pathway. These are actually physical connections where extensions (axons) from brain cells (neurons) are stimulated to connect with branching (dendrites) from other cells.

Every connection that is used often becomes strengthened. Over time the axon becomes myelinated (insulated). That allows it to work easier and faster. And that makes it more likely to become a habit. Your old reading strategies have been reinforced over the years. The pathways are strong. It's OK to leave those strong pathways. You don't need to try to break them up.

To form a new habit, it simply takes three steps.

1. Think about doing it correctly.
2. Do it correctly.
3. Do it correctly often.

That's right, every time you even *think* of speed reading successfully, it increases your chances of making it happen.

Perfect Practice Key 1: Practice Thinking

You've heard how successful Olympic athletes use mental practice to succeed? That's called visualization. You can apply that same skill to speed reading. Since practice makes permanent, what you think about the most will become what you get.

Never think about missing something or failing at it. Begin now to think about reading successfully. Think about getting all you want. Now think about recalling all you want. Also think about getting great pleasure out of it. Every day invest two minutes to mentally practice succeeding at reading.

When it's appropriate, close your eyes and see yourself reading quickly, always succeeding at it. You can mentally see yourself from a distance as if you were a third party looking at you, a great reader. Watch as that person (you) reads quickly with great understanding.

Now shift the focus. Instead of your mind's eye being across the room, move it to the eyes of the actual reader (you). Now you are seeing what the reader would be seeing as he or she (you) actually reads fast. It's a whole different experience from the previous visualization. It requires more focus and attention, but it pays off.

Practice speed reading whatever material you have to read the most often. Practice this at least one to two minutes a day. You may want to break it up into four segments of 30 seconds each. The critical ingredient is to think about doing it successfully so that you are creating the habit mentally as well as physically.

Remember the more pathways you make in your brain that are positive and strong, the easier it becomes for you to think those same thoughts again. Practice makes permanent. What you think about the most will become what you get.

Perfect Practice Key 2: Use Your Peripheral Vision

Everyone has peripheral vision—it's what we see on the edges of our main focus. It's not the center, but the outer boundaries of a panorama.

Your peripheral vision is critical to reading faster. It allows you to pick up an extraordinary amount of information with little work or awareness. It's like another world.

To develop this ability, look out the window. Now, allow your gaze to relax and soften, seeing no detail. Just take in the whole outdoor scene or picture at once. This is the type of relaxed big vision that you'll want to use in reading fast. In your normal life, most of the time you use your big vision (like a wide-angle lens in a camera) or you look at something in detail (like looking through a narrowed telephoto lens).

To practice better reading skills, you'll want to get good at consciously changing that wide to narrow to wide focus. You'll want to get skilled in doing it upon will; to go back and forth between a condensed, narrow, and concentrated focus to a wider, all-encompassing focus. Practice this at school, work, or play. You want the habit, not just the occasional conscious ability but the automated habit of being able to see how you want to see at will. Go ahead and practice this now. You may want to do this every day, whenever you think of it.

Here's another exercise. Extend your arms out in

front of you with the palms together. Begin wiggling your fingers, while at the same time moving your hands further away from each other and out to the sides. Stop moving your hands when you can no longer see your wiggling fingers at all with your peripheral vision. How far apart were your arms when you reached the limit of your peripheral vision? What was your marking point? Have you ever seen a page larger than that huge area? Of course not. Your peripheral vision is capable of scanning large areas. Next time, do your best to exceed your original marking point. Practice this at least once a day.

Perfect Practice Key 3: Vertical Practice

Use this section to practice the exercises recommended. Relax and breathe slowly and deeply while you do this. The Evelyn Wood Speed Reading Program, which has taught over a million students, demonstrated that by using your hand properly you can increase reading speed and comprehension. You may use your finger or your entire hand. Simply put your finger under the words that you are reading. Move it along from left to right at a comfortable speed. Keep it moving. Pick up your finger at the end of each line and quickly move it to the next line.

If you want to use your entire hand and go even faster, place your hand on the page. Spread your fingers and relax your hand. Now move it smoothly across and down the page and follow it with your eyes.

Stay focused on the print and allow the meaning to come to you. Your eyes will need some practice following this new object on the page. Most new speed readers need to practice anywhere from two to twenty hours before they are really comfortable with this new way of reading.

Move your eyes to pause for a split second just above the center of each line. Use a relaxed, soft focus—the kind that allows you to look off into a distance to view the horizon. Keeping your eyes still, take in the words on both sides. Then move down to the next line and do the same. Simply fix your eyes just above the center word and see the rest of the words around it. Spend no longer than one second on each line. Soon, you may notice your eyes beginning to adjust to this. Keep your focus softly at the center of each line. You'll find that it will soon become easy for you to grasp the whole line visually at one time. Occasionally, your eyes may want to shift to the old back and forth process. If so, break your eyes away, look off in the distance, relax your eyes, and look back again with the soft focus.

If you have some challenges or frustration with this exercise at first, relax. Repeat it several times. With practice you will be able to master all the exercises. Stay patient with yourself and you will make healthy progress each time you practice. Little by little, you'll develop the skills you want.

Perfect Practice Key 4: Speed Practice

Are you ready for some fun speed boosters? You've watched a TV, video, or CD-ROM before. Did you know that each of those is recorded one frame image at a time? Typically the single frames are about 24–30 per second. Somehow they become a live, moving whole when they appear on the screen. This is because your brain is taking in the fast sequence of pictures so quickly, it cannot stop to create a thought about one of them. The meaning of the visual is not in a single frame, it's in the whole package.

In the same way, as you move your eyes down the page, instead of left to right, word by word, you'll experience something different. You will experience the printed material as a continuous whole. You will soon be able to quickly and easily take in bigger chunks of material. The more the amount of material and the faster you process it, the greater the movie or TV effect your brain gets.

To learn how to do this, you'll need the use of both hands and a large book. Flatten out the book, creasing the center down to make it easy to turn pages. Start at the beginning. Flip through the pages of the book quickly, turning the right-hand page from the top corner with your left hand. Next, pull your eyes down the page by using your other hand as a guide. Use your right hand with palm down, fingers slightly spread. It looks a bit like you're brushing down each page with your right hand. Your fingers should be extended and relaxed. Start at the top of each page and brush it down. Allow your eyes to follow your hand down each page trying to see as many words as possible.

Start by brushing each page in two or three seconds, gradually reducing the time spent on each page until you can go as fast as you can turn pages. The goal is not just to get a maximum page-burning hyper speed. The real goal is to train your eyes to move comfortably down a page as well as in the traditional left-to-right method, and train your eyes to use the softer, wider, more relaxed focus that allows your peripheral vision to take in more words at a time.

Pace yourself, starting at 20 pages a minute, slowly increasing to 50 or even 100 pages a minute as your skills increase. There are many variations on this exercise that you can try.

You might want to use different postures, different chairs, new lighting, or try a new book. You may also want to put on some fast, upbeat music. Many readers find that instrumental music works better than music with words. How much fun might it be with the theme from the *Lone Ranger* ("William Tell Overture") by Rossini?

You also might enjoy using different patterns with your hand going down the page. The first one suggested was simply going from top to bottom. Often a U shape works well, going down the left-hand page and back up the right-hand page. Are you concerned that you're looking or reading *up* the page? Relax. It's just a motor exercise for the eyes and hand to get into new patterns of learning.

Do these exercises with your own variations every day. They take just a couple of minutes and they'll bring you great rewards. What makes them fun is that you can do them even if you're a bit tired. There's no reading, it's just a way to help form new habits.

When you've read the preceding section, check this box. You're one step closer to your goal!

Perfect Practice Key 5: Comprehension Practice

(A quick reminder: Are you taking frequent breaks to relax your eyes? Are you doing the palming exercises? This will reduce eye strain and allow you to enjoy this process of developing your capabilities.)

Pick an easy book with big print and lots of bold headings or graphics. You would teach your child to swim, not in a dangerous ocean but in a safe lake or shallow pool. In the same way, when you are learning new skills you want to enjoy the success of the process. You'll get the hang of it and succeed much quicker with fun, simple, and easy material.

Read the title and anything from the front or back covers. Pick up any other information with a quick browse. Read the back cover or jacket summary. This is an excellent way to get a sense of the book. Read the table of contents. This is the outline and structure of the book. You will learn how many chapters there are and how long they run. This can help you begin to get a feeling for the book. In fact, you may become interested in one or more chapters just through the browse. Now that you're a bit familiar with the book, we can start the real practice of developing comprehension.

Comprehension at high speed is similar to that at low speed. The one difference is the scale of time. If you read very slowly and you lose attention or focus for 20 seconds, you've lost only a couple of sentences or a paragraph. At greater speeds, 20 seconds may be as much as two to five pages. Now that's quite a difference! You can tell that means one of two things: either you've got to increase your concentration skills or read faster for short bursts, then pause. We'll use both of those suggestions to build our comprehension at greater speeds.

This exercise is called a talk-along. Since you'll be talking, you'll want to find a place where you have privacy and can do it without distractions. Put your book in front of you and begin turning pages and brushing each page with your open hand, palm down, just as you did in the speed practice in Key 4. Get a smooth rhythm going, just looking at columns of print, for three to four seconds a page. So far, it's just a speed exercise.

Here's where it becomes a comprehension builder. As you bring your eyes quickly down each page, practice using your soft, relaxed, big picture focus. Look at nothing in particular, just big areas of the page. Keep turning pages and add one new dimension: talking. Describe, out loud, what you see on the page. Is it big print or small print? Are there graphics, pictures, or bold print? Say so: "There's big print... there is a lot of description now..." You'll say if there's a narrative or a dialogue. Can you recognize the topic from any clues? If so, say so, out loud.

This is a simple drill and yet it trains your brain to do many important things at once: move quickly down a page; use the relaxed, soft focus; stay focused on the page; and formulate, out loud, what you are seeing while you are seeing it. It's a terrific comprehension builder. The beauty of this is that you are only describing general impressions of what's on the page—no reading allowed. Practice this generalizing drill and soon your talking along will develop into comprehending along. All it takes is practice. The brain learns the essence of focused concentration with comprehension and with speed. Because practice makes permanent here are two suggestions.

1. Make sure you practice this the proper way.
2. Make sure you practice.

Speed reading means that you've gathered a lot of information in a short time. However, your brain needs a way to sort it, store it, and use it. Every time you read, you need to do something active with the information as soon as you finish. You can summarize to yourself, tell another person, write it down, or mind map it.

You now have the foundation for reading faster. There are two more things to do:

1. Go back and actually practice what you just learned, doing it once a day.
2. Read the second half of the speed reading session coming up in the next chapter.

If you're ready for faster reading, jump in and get started.

Review

Once you have finished this, today's assignment is done. Before you close this book and move on to something else, let's review what you accomplished:

✓ You made the decision to continue the program.
✓ You read the check-in statement.
✓ You learned strategies on how to read faster.
✓ You know the skill will take work to achieve—using it beats practicing it.
✓ You read your review for the day (that's this list).

 Congratulations! You have completed Day 8 of your 30 days. Close the book and we'll see you tomorrow!

SPEED READING

Day 9

✔ **Check-in**

First, did you finish yesterday's section on speed reading? If not, get to it, because once you've learned to read faster, the whole rest of this book will get easier. Then you can start here and continue that topic. Be warned, though. You are probably going to have to spend more than 30 minutes on this section. We have a *lot* of material to cover.

SPEED READING, PART II

You'll get to the part on reading faster in just a few moments. But first, learn to read smarter. Here are strategies to boost your comprehension. Use each one as you see fit.

Hot Tip 1: Set a Purpose Before You Start

Create a reason to read. A reading purpose and time management are inseparable. In the information age, we can no longer presume to read every document at the same speed or level of comprehension. Not only is this impossible, but with the amount of material we need to read, it is not even desirable. When you establish your purpose, the real power of your brain comes immediately into play.

As a nice fringe benefit, creating a purpose releases the vise grip of guilt—guilt about violating those long-time rules about how we are supposed to read. Your inner voice may express this guilt by saying, "I bought this magazine, so even if I don't *want* to read all the articles, I ought to, otherwise I wasted my money!" Or, "I spent ten bucks on this book, I at least ought to get my money's worth by spending a long time reading it."

With a better sense of purpose, you can justify putting aside the material you do not need to read. You'll be better able to throw out, reassess, or give away those publications that waste your valuable time.

Establishing a prereading purpose takes as little as five seconds. But over the course of a lifetime, the savings to you in time, guilt, and convenience can be huge. This simple strategy is so critical and far-reaching that it can instantly and permanently change your relationship with and results in reading.

When we clarify our purpose, we greatly increase the odds of reaching it. Purpose focuses energy and attention. Give your mind a clear focus and purpose, and almost anything can be accomplished. In fact, your purpose is the driving force behind all reading. Examples of diversity in purpose include:

♦ **For a textbook:** Become detail literate. Get a solid background in both the overview and the specifics. Read it on several levels. Recall needed: moderate to high. Pleasure desired: irrelevant. End product: learn enough to be able to write about it, converse on it, and pass tests on it.

♦ **For a magazine:** Build on areas of interest. Add something new. Find all articles that relate to your interests. Recall needed: low to moderate. Pleasure desired: moderate to high. End product: highlight key ideas or tear them out and enter into your to-do list.

♦ **For a distraction only:** Your purpose could be non-productive. For instance, your main purpose for reading in the doctor's waiting room may be to occupy your time, simply a distraction. This can be, at times, just as legitimate a purpose as reading for a test you have to pass.

♦ **For a newspaper:** The broad update. Get a quick update on local, national, and international stories. Enjoy your favorite comics. Check for local TV listings. Read any interesting people or sports stories. Recall needed: low. Pleasure desired: moderate. End product: learn just enough to feel like you're keeping up with daily events.

So, before you ever read anything again, pause. Figure out why you are reading what you're reading. Then let that purpose drive your strategies.

Hot Tip 2: Bring Out What You Already Know

Before you start reading, trigger or surface as much background as you already have on that topic. This primes the brain to generate more interest and meaning as you read. It's almost like Velcro. You provide one half of it, the material provides the other half, and bingo, they connect!

There are many ways you can do this priming process. Get out a piece of paper and write out everything you know about the topic already. You can do it in a list format or you can use an organized pattern like the visual maps introduced in Day 5. You can also brainstorm this topic out loud in a study group or with a friend. The main purpose is to stimulate past related learning.

Hot Tip 3: Ask Questions Before Reading

You'll have two categories of questions. The first category is process and value questions. They help you stand back and identify what you need and want from the material. Here are examples of questions that can and should form part of your prereading habit.

➤ What is my final application of this reading material?

➤ How important is this material to me? What specifically is the value of it?

➤ What are the key points?

➤ Do I want to recall specific facts and other details?

The second category of questions you'll ask are more content related. In order to be able to ask powerful prereading questions, you'll want to scan the material very quickly first. You'll be looking for the author's key ideas and trigger words. How do you identify those key or trigger words? It's easier than you think.

Have you ever noticed while you were reading certain words seemed to jump off the page and ask for attention? There's a good chance that those words are key to the author's message. Those words have an urgency. "Hey, look at me," they seem to say. Those trigger words are easy to spot, repeatedly used terms that present themes, vocabulary, and central ideas. They are the ones that help you draw meaning from the material.

You can turn those trigger words into questions for maximum benefit. Go quickly through the material to locate or discover anything that prompts your brain for a question (see Browsing, Day 4). The possibilities include

- anything with bullets.
- anything with titles.
- all the subtitles.
- table of contents.
- headings.
- subheadings.
- front and back covers.
- first and last pages of the book.
- copyright date.
- index.
- text in boldface or italics.
- first and last paragraphs of any sections.
- sections and material in boxes.
- any figures or charts.
- chapter summaries.
- previews or review questions.
- anything that catches your attention.

You'll learn a great deal by scanning and asking questions. It seems like it's not useful for real learning, but it is. You'll learn three types of information.

1. key content ideas
2. the basic structure of the material
3. thousands of words, ideas, or meanings that were picked up subconsciously through your peripheral vision

At times, you will literally find everything you want to know just through this scanning process. That's one of the unexpected joys of prereading. You'll learn what to expect, where to look for important information. In time, this scanning step will become the most valued part of your overall reading process.

Hot Tip 4: Use the Layered Learning Process

Acquire different kinds of understanding at different times in the book. If you ask your brain to get specific about just one thing, comprehension is more likely to happen. If it's a novel that you are reading just for fun, pick up the book and start reading from page one to the end. Why just one layer? Your accountability is low for understanding, meaning, and recall. However, if you were required to read a novel for a class, you'd need more than pleasure from reading. You would have to change your approach. Because you would need specific information from your reading, you would have to approach the material in a different manner. Your studying might be layered like this.

♦ First, scan the whole book. Get a basic overview, meet the characters and notice the settings.

♦ Then go back and read it for the full plot and details. Stop every few pages and jot down what's going on. That will save you from having to go back later.

Textbooks demand additional steps. If you are reading a textbook or an article, you could layer your information-gathering like this:

♦ First, a brief overview of titles, subtitles, and visual aids. This scanning step might take five minutes. Then you can start to map out the structure on a visual map.

♦ Question asking time (no answers yet): Turn the topic sentences and key words into questions you'd like to get answered later.

♦ The main material (all the details): Here, you'll read for your best understanding and meaning, but not to memorize.

♦ Review for anything unclear. In this last step, you'll reaffirm what you know, but more important, you'll make sure you have everything you want.

Layering the reading includes prereading. This is a casual browse before reading for your best comprehension. It has some advantages. It promotes long-term memory because of repetition. It helps you comprehend and categorize the material you read. It encourages you to build a mental structure of what you read. Any material you actively organize, you will remember longer.

The whole concept of prereading often leaves many readers discouraged or skeptical. They feel it's just too much extra work or, "If speed reading's so great, why do we need to preread something?" Here is a quick reality check.

Reality Check: Prereading doesn't add time, it saves time. Think of your reading requirements as not how many minutes or seconds per page, but time per project. While a traditional slower reader may read something over once formally, they'll often make the time to go back to reread something they missed again and again. That rereading is dismissed as, "Of course you go back; you just need to." What counts is this: "Is the total time, from start to finish any less for you to get what you needed out of your reading?" With prereading, the answer is usually yes.

Reality Check: It's not a waste, it's very valuable. Prereading allows your mind to do several things.

1. Get a mental map of the material before reading it.
2. Discover what you know and don't know ahead of time.
3. Plant some seeds for new ideas.
4. Find your way around faster.
5. Better understand what you're being exposed to.
6. Help you figure out what you want to know.
7. Feel more confident about what you're learning through repetition.

Yet in spite of how valuable prereading is, there are times when you don't want to preread. These include reading a letter from a friend, a suspenseful or dramatic novel, or poetry. But for the vast majority of your reading, you'll want to do the prereading process.

Reality Check: It's the way your brain is designed to learn. The more you know about a text before you actually read it, the easier it will be to read. Research suggests that your brain works better with small pieces of information. We make sense out of ideas that we have heard before, not wild, out-of-the-blue ideas. The human brain functions poorly when trying to grasp an idea or concept that is totally foreign to it.

Have you ever tried to explain a big new idea or novel concept to a friend? It's tough! He usually listens, then when you're done, says something like, "Well, I'm sure it's a good idea, but I just don't get it." His brain just doesn't have the existing connections or networks to create any meaning out of it. The secret to preparing the brain for better comprehension, meaning, and recall at a high rate is prereading. It provides the patterns, the hooks, the vocabulary, the map, the questions, and the overview that makes for better reading. Prereading is simple and critical to your success.

Hot Tip 5: Organize What You Read

Our minds seem to remember things better when they *belong* somewhere. As an example, the ten items from a grocery list are better recalled when they are divided into the sections and aisles of a store like fruits, frozen foods, dairy, vegetables, canned goods, meats, household products. The same is true in your understanding and recall of text material. Find or invent appropriate categories for storing your material. Here are a few ways to organize ideas:

- people, places, events, conflicts
- chapter titles and subtitles

- concept, example, application
- who, what, how, why, when, where
- themes and movements
- purpose, method, results
- problem, analysis, solution

Hot Tip 6: Write as You Read

Once you begin to read, learn to pause, every half page, and write down key ideas, thoughts, and facts. You might add the information to a visual map. Keep the information useful to you. Add pictures, drawings, or illustrations to what you write down. The colors and doodles that you add to your mind map will help your brain understand and remember it better. For examples of these visual maps, see Day 5.

Hot Tip 7: Learn to Maintain Relaxed Alertness

The best frame of mind and body (or state) is that of relaxed alertness. It could also be called casual focus. Notice that these phrases are a paradox—to be both focused and relaxed. Yet that is the optimum, perfect, ideal state for reading. Too tense and you miss out. Too relaxed and you miss out. To get into this state, it takes some practice. It's like the zone in sports. When an athlete is in the zone his or her performance is at the peak, yet it's not hard work.

You might reread the chapters on motivation and concentration. They give dozens of strategies on how to boost concentration and get your brain in gear. In speed reading, you'll need greater concentration and focus, but you'll need it for a shorter period of time.

Hot Tip 8: Get Help from Many Sources

If you need help with your reading beyond what this book provides, go get it! Mastering this skill is critical to your success. You can get tutoring, seek help from a professor, take a class, purchase a course on CD-ROM, or get information from another book.

☐ When you've read the preceding section, check this box. You're one step closer to your goal!

SEVEN KEYS TO READING FASTER

Key 1: Begin with an *I Can* Attitude

Listen to comments you make about reading and comprehension. Never again make jokes about yourself, your ability, or the subject. Avoid joking about speed reading. It's a skill you can and will master. Quit saying how fat a book is or complaining about how long it'll take to read. Start telling yourself that you *can* read better. Feel confident when it's time to read, knowing you have new tools to work with.

Key 2: Get Your Brain Ready to Read

Here's the ideal, and you should get as close to it as you can: Cool temperature for reading (68–70 degrees), no distractions, pleasant smells, good background music (if any at all), pleasing surroundings, and a comfortable chair. Make sure you've had a drink of water first.

Sit up with your back either straight or leaning back.

Sit at a table and rest the book as high as you comfort-ably can. Prop it up if you need to, and angle it so that the book faces you directly. This decreases the strain on your eyes, and makes your brain want to keep looking. Take a two-minute stretch or get a drink of water every 20–30 minutes.

Set goals for how much time you want to spend and what you want to get out of the reading. Here's an example.

> I have 20 pages to read. I will do this in ten min-utes. I want to learn the seven keys to speed reading.

If you really want to reach your goal and if you are motivated, you'll reach it.

Key 3: Vary Your Speed Depending on Content

Read light, fun fiction quickly. Read new, unfamiliar textbooks several times, first at a fast speed, then again at a medium speed. Read heartthrob novels the slowest of all. Speed readers change their speed all the time.

Your goal is to spend less total time in a book. Sometimes the best way to do that is to read a 20-page textbook chapter three times (once each at 1,000, 2,000, and 5,000 words per minute) instead of just once at 250 words a minute (one-half of a textbook page a minute). The first option takes you 17 minutes, leaving you 13 more to add to your notes for a total of 30 minutes. The second option takes you 40 minutes and that's with no notes!

Key 4: Read with a Guide

There are several habits that slow reading down to a crawl. Obviously daydreaming and losing interest are common ones. But more common are habits like rereading and regression. These habits constitute from 10–50 percent of all the time you spend reading. That means that up to half of the time that you think you're reading, you're not! You're going backwards or staring into space. These habits can be beaten with some help— your help.

As a child, you put your fingertips on the page to follow the words without even thinking about what you were doing. It helped you concentrate better. It's still a good idea to use your hand or a pencil to read with as a guide. There are two reasons: First, you won't read the same line over again or skip a line, both of which can take up nearly half of all reading time. Second, it makes reading active. The movement of your hand or pencil helps you concentrate.

Read for meaning, not words. When you read quickly, your brain scans for information and sorts out what you want and what you don't. No more reading word by word, line by line. Let your hand float down the page and, if it helps, keep asking yourself the question, "What's going on? What's happening on this page?"

Key 5: Practice Makes Permanent

If you want to read faster, you need to use your new skills. Hoping won't work and grueling practices alone won't either. There are two simple ways to become good at speed reading. First, just do it—jump in and use the skills you're learning. Second, practice it. Keep your practice simple and fun. The right kind of practice trains your brain to start seeing whole word groups and meaning groups. The practice time you'll need is just five minutes a day. The rest of the practice you'll get will be the real thing. Using the skill will make it permanent.

Here's a simple exercise you can do. Get a big, thick textbook. Sit in your psyched up power reading position and get ready to blast off. Have a clock with a second hand or a timer next to you.

Start at the beginning of the book, turn pages, and use your hand to pull your eyes down each page. It's as if you are brushing down the pages with your hand. Make your movements smooth and rhythmical. Turn, brush, turn, brush. Don't read, just let your eyes get used to seeing the page quickly, moving down and following your hand. Your goal is 60 pages in one minute. If you can do better, great. Do this for one minute. You want to get increasingly smoother at turning pages and seeing the words better without any reading.

Next, repeat the above exercise for two minutes. You'll still aim for 60 pages a minute, but this time add sound: talk out loud about what you see. You might say, "I see a new chapter just started, there's a blank page, there's a graph about something, there's a bunch of subtitles, there's a list of some kind . . ."

This trains your mind to understand more at higher speeds. Do this exercise every day. The best books to use are the same books you have to read for school. Practice with them over and over. You get two benefits for the effort of one: while your reading speed improves, so does your awareness of the material in the books.

For the last minute of your five minutes practice, simply find the beginning of a chapter. Then time yourself for one minute. Read as quickly as you can for good understanding. After your minute is up, measure how far you read. Count in quarter pages. Did you do three-fourths of a page? Great! Two pages? Three and one-half? One-half? Whatever you did, congratulate yourself! It will get better every day.

In this chapter you've learned the strategies for comprehension and speed. You've learned the skills for practice, too. There are five critical areas to practice: mental practice, peripheral practice, vertical practice, speed practice, and comprehension practice. They are each essential to the total package of skills called speed reading. You'll want to commit yourself to practice each of them every day. About two minutes of each equals ten minutes a day. That's a small price to pay for the rewards of a lifetime. In this information age, you'll need everything you can get.

SCHEDULING

Schedules can be either a pain in the neck or a blessing. It's up to you to make them a blessing. Let's face it—you need to know what's coming up, and when. You need to keep a schedule for important reasons. The secret to a useful calendar is to know what to put on it and to use it.

First Easy Step

First, get a calendar or date book. Fill in all the usual important stuff, like holidays, tests, and vacations. Now get ready to make your schedule work for you; wherever you have tests scheduled, go backwards and schedule three study-time slots. You'll only need two of them, but that way, you're covered if one of them gets cancelled due to an emergency (like a party!).

Now comes the important part. Use the calendar to make decisions. If you want to do something on a weekend, check your calendar. If it looks like you can spare the time to go out on Friday night then do it! But if you want to go out on Sunday night, check what you've got coming up that week and ask yourself if you're allowing enough study time.

☑ If you already have a calendar that you've been using, check this box.

☐ If you don't have a calendar and will get one now, check this box.

When will you get a calendar? _____

Where? _____

MEET YOUR PROFESSORS

Professors are your first source of help at school and, obviously, the ones who give the grades. The better you know them, the better the relationship and the more ways you can help each other.

First Easy Step

1. **Listen well in class.** It shows you care and can help you understand the professor's mind-set better at testing or grade time. That will give you the key information you need. If your professor is a really impulsive, off-the-wall person, you can be more creative. If not, you'd better be more conventional and follow the rules.

2. **Ask professors what their favorite subjects, authors, books, and topics are.** I once had a professor who was a notoriously hard grader. I asked him who his favorite author was and favorite books were. I then did my research papers on his favorite authors. I worked hard, but it was worth it. I got an A in the class.

3. **Learn the rules.** Ask the professor how much you are expected to talk, ask, or contribute in class. Ask what you should do if you can't turn an assignment in on time. Ask if there are any outside sources for tutoring, or helpful resources on video, computers, or in the library.

☐ Check this box if your professor knows you by name.

If not, when will you introduce yourself? _____

Review

Once you have finished this, today's assignment is finished. Before you close the book and move on to something else, let's review what you accomplished.

✓ You made the decision to continue the program.
✓ You read the check-in statement.
✓ You continued to learn how to read faster.
✓ You learned the importance of keeping a schedule.
✓ You realized how important it is for professors to know you.
✓ You read your review for the day (that's this list).

 Congratulations! You have completed Day 9 of your 30 days. Close the book and we'll see you tomorrow!

Day 10

AMAZING MEMORY POWER

Instead of failing to remember, you can amaze yourself with your ability to recall. You can remember much more of what you learn. To do that, it will take a few things. First, you'll want to understand how your brain's memory systems work. Second, you'll want to learn some specific strategies for how to trigger the release of the material when you want it. Third, you'll want to begin to use the ideas. By themselves, they're only tools. As you begin to implement these ideas, you'll literally be astonished at how much you can recall of what you read.

Your Brain's Three Memory Systems

There are many ways to classify your memory (for example, short-term and long-term, active and passive, surface and repressed, positive and negative). While there is no single location in the brain marked off for each of these, the brain clearly acts as if it has three systems:

1.   categorical memory
2.   body memory—procedural (motor) and sensory
3.   episodic memory

Can you identify the one you use the most?

Categorical Memory

This type of memory is for words, facts, names, and other text. It's unnatural and requires constant practice to keep fresh. That's why most people have the experience of forgetting so much trivia. The brain is simply not designed to recall that type of infor- mation. Pro- fessors who require a large recall of text- book informa- tion are, at best, develop- ing self-disci- pline in the learners. It is certainly not the only or best way to learn the content. This type of memory requires strong activation by

the learner to succeed. It requires rehearsal, it's resistant to change, isolated from context, has strict quantity limits, often lacks meaning, and is linked to extrinsic motivation. It is limited by chunk size (we can recall items in groups up to seven chunks). It is the only memory that has both a short (about 15 seconds long) and long term.

In short, the main reason that you forget so much of what you read (whether reading fast or slowly) is that the human brain was never designed to recall large volumes of print material. In fact there's no record of writing (and hence, reading) until only recently in our geologic past (about 5,000 years ago). But fortunately, there are ways to recall what you read. We'll get to those possibilities in a moment.

Procedural and Sensory Memory

Motor memory, often called procedural (for example, riding a bicycle), musical memory (the melody of a favorite song), and sensory memory (smell of a flower) is processed very differently. The material learned this way is highly likely to be recalled. These are, in fact, the most commonly used methods for early childhood learning. A child's life is full of actions that require standing, riding, sitting, trying out, eating, moving, playing, building, or running. The learning is then embedded in the body and remembered for much longer.

We are physical and sensory learners. Movement, action, role playing, drama, music, and sports all are easier to recall than a page of print. The brain is also very effective in recalling any particularly strong, emotionally triggering event. Examples include a funeral, a birthday, a car wreck, a snake in the face, a first date, an unusual sound, first kiss, a scream, a special perfume or cologne.

Episodic Memory

So far we have talked about memory that is activated by words (categorical) or by actions (motor). Our episodic memory is activated by where we are when we learn something (locations). The formation of this natural memory is motivated by curiosity, novelty, and expectations. It's enhanced by intensified sensory input (sights, sounds, smells, taste, touch). The information is stored in a visual fabric or weave of mental space. It's a thematic map of the intellectual landscape, where learning and memory is prompted by changes in location or circumstances.

This memory works because our brain's visual system sorts by both content (what) and context (where). You see and experience everything in a context (location and circumstances). What did you have for dinner last night? To answer that question, you might first ask yourself, "Where was I?" The location gives you clues to the answer. In school, the room your class is in (location) will often remind you of what (content) was learned. Students who took finals in rooms that were not where they heard the course lectures did worse than those who took the exam in the same room. How do you turn these three types of memory into practical strategies? Let's turn to the specifics.

SEVEN SECRETS TO GREAT RECALL

Believe in Yourself

Much of today's brain research indicates that we store nearly everything we experience. When we forget, it's a performance problem. Recall is thus a matter of learning the appropriate tools, context, or strategies to retrieve information we've learned.

Use the Right System

Your brain has three memory systems, as mentioned earlier. Use the system that best fits what you're trying to do. Remember that your memory is context (location) and state (mood) dependent. Information is either stored in your mind (categorical), in your body (procedural/motor), or in space (episodic). Let's say you have a great deal of facts to recall. You'll use the categorical memory processing system.

Here's how. Link key areas of the material to your body parts (mentally associate them). Link one item to your fingers, another to your wrist, another to your elbow, and so on. You may also use the rooms of your house. Link key points things you see when you walk into your apartment, dorm, or home. Maybe it's the sofa first, then the TV, a lamp, a picture on the wall, then the kitchen. Practice that for two minutes, several times a day for several days until you're sure you've got it. Then, whenever you have material to recall for a lecture, presentation, exam, or meeting, simply associate each point with one of the items or places.

Plan to Remember

Be strong in your intention to remember. This means that ahead of time you'll decide what you want to learn, how well you need it, and what you're likely to need for recall. Study in a place where you have all the tools for best understanding and recall.

Understand State Dependency

Our memory is state dependent. The same physiological or emotional state you're in while you learn is the ideal state in which to test for that information. If you study while you're happy and take a test while you're stressed, you won't perform well. The solution is simple. You have only minimal control over the learning states; your teacher influences part of those. However, studying is different. Do your best to match your studying state with your testing state. If you know you'll be stressed out at test time, study with a timer and give yourself short deadlines.

Use Your Memory

Researchers agree our memory works on the use-it-or-lose-it principle. So, exercise your memory and it will serve you well. You can extend short-term memory into long-term only by activating it. It takes thinking, using, consolidating, and practicing to embed information in your mind.

Be Selective

You rarely need to remember everything you read. You often need to recall key concepts, meaning, relationships, and facts. Avoid wasting your time trying to recall all material you come across—there's too much. Learn to prioritize and you can succeed at the key areas. It makes more sense to know where to find information than to use up all your time on memorizing all or most of what you read. Information becomes obsolete quickly. Simply learn where you can go for the newest material rather than storing old material.

Review and Review Again

Unfortunately, there's a difference between memory and recall. We may store a great deal in our memory, but without the ability to recall, it's frustrating. Our ability to recall drops dramatically unless we review information to reinforce. In fact, within a month, 80 percent of what you've learned is likely to be forgotten. But when material is reviewed periodically, retention can be almost perfect. The review strengthens the neural networks created by learning the new material and makes it more available for long-term memory.

Review your material three ways. First, as you read material you want to remember, stop and summarize or mind map what you are reading. You'll learn about mental maps in just a moment. Connect it to what has come before or to the context of your study. This simple act of constant summarizing is one of the most powerful tools for learning and remembering.

Second, review the material often. Research recommends that you review for two minutes within the following times: first within the first 60 minutes of learning it, then within 24 hours of learning it, then within seven days of learning it, then within 30 days of learning it.

This totals up to eight minutes per month. Ignore this review and expect to have a scattered, sloppy, and fragmented recall that leads only to frustration. Invest this time and reap the efforts for months.

The third step is to take purposeful breaks in your learning sessions. Doing so works in harmony with our understanding of how our brain works.

- You remember most from the first and last part of your study session.
- You remember most any learning that was temporarily interrupted.

You may want to takes breaks anywhere from 20 to 45 minutes apart. A good length for a break is 5 to 15 minutes.

USE VISUAL MAPS

Visual maps were introduced in Day 5: Note Taking. The most obvious use of these maps is for taking original notes on books, articles, lectures, and meetings. In addition, you can use them to retrieve stored information from time to time. In studying for an exam, preparing to deliver a talk, and any time you need a review of information, a glance at a mind map gives you a quick summary of all the essential points in just a few seconds—far less time than reading through paragraphs or pages of notes.

There are many ways for you to remember what you've learned. All of these take some time and effort. But the price of not doing them is that you'll end up with the same old thing: forgotten material. Take just a few moments and pick the following ideas that suit you best. Here are some of the best ways to help recall learned material:

♦ Use the double-entry method: write key ideas on the left-hand page and use the right-hand for colorful illustrations, symbols, doodles, or pictures.

♦ Repeat the key ideas within 10 minutes after learning them, then 48 hours later, and then seven days later.

♦ Make a concrete reminder, like an object, token, or artifact.

♦ Capture your ideas before they fade out by recording them on a pocket microcassette recorder.

♦ Use acrostics (first letter of each key word forms a new word). As a kid you may have used this to memorize the names of the planets with the sentence, "My Very Excellent Mother Just Sells Nuts Until Passover" (Mercury, Venus, Earth, . . . Pluto). You may also have learned the musical notes on the lines of the G-clef by memorizing "Every Good Boy Does Fine." Learn the Great Lakes by making one word of their first letters: HOMES (Huron, Ontario, Michigan, Erie, Superior).

- Put the overview on a large, colorful picture or poster. Add symbols or personal doodles. Post it for review.

- Organize your material in idea groups of seven or less to make each group of data easy to recall.

- Create acronyms for main ideas.

Here are a few more ideas you might find useful to build strong recall.

- Review using all five senses: hearing, sight, smell, taste, and touch.

- Use storyboards (like oversized cartoon or comic strip panels) of your key ideas. Review them often.

- Make a video or audiotape that is related to the key ideas from your material. The more fun you have, the better.

- Transfer key ideas to your computer and refer to them often.

- Create or redo a song; rewrite the lyrics of an old favorite, make a rap out of the key terms or ideas.

- Increase your reading accountability: ask yourself to review or check your understanding at regular reading intervals—maybe every five minutes or ten pages, whichever comes first.

- Reality review: Go to the place, if possible, where the material you're learning occurs. It might be a museum, downtown, a park, or office building. This will help you get a better visual imprint.

- Make the content more relevant and important by finding a way that it can be used in your personal life.

♦ Summarize. In your own words, sum up what you are learning or have just learned. Teaching the information will invite you to clarify it in your own mind, and the repetition will boost understanding and recall.

♦ Follow up your reading with journal writing. Give yourself enough time for useful reflection (at least 15 minutes).

Final suggestions

♦ Build a working model that embodies the key elements of the main ideas presented.

♦ Put key ideas on cards. Group and regroup them. Sort your learning into categories. The active involvement in organizing the material can provide meaningful patterns and associations that help recall.

♦ Create or support some kind of learner study support group for review.

♦ Practice better nutrition; in several studies, mineral supplements or the lecithin from wheat germ helped. (See also Eat Smart at Day 15.)

♦ Create a strong positive association with the material. Engage your emotions through drama or debate.

♦ Make up a story utilizing the key facts or ideas. It supplies a meaningful context for the material and the plot provides an associative thread of ideas such that one triggers the next.

♦ Use strong sensory associations to strengthen the memory.

- Make a mental map of it or a mind map to share with a friend. Then redo it later on.
- Teach the concepts to a roommate for review.
- Do a follow-up a month later by reviewing the material and using video, writing, or a talk.
- Learn each chapter or section of a book in different places so each location is a key clue to the content.

When you've read the preceding section, check this box. You're one step closer to your goal!

TURN FAILURES INTO SUCCESSES

It would be great never to make mistakes, but you've made them before and you'll make them again. But what if every failure is the seed for a success? We think we know what's good and bad, but we never really know. In Chinese, the symbol for the word *crisis* is the same as the one for *opportunity*. Maybe the Chinese know something we don't know!

First Easy Step

Think of something that happened to you that seemed bad at the time. Then think of something positive that came out of it. For example, let's say that you just broke up with your girlfriend or boyfriend. Bad news, it seems. At the time of the break up, the other person seemed perfect. But in time, you may discover that there's someone who is better for you. Repeat this exercise as often as needed to change your attitude from negative to positive.

Now be ready. The next time something bad happens, you can moan and groan for awhile. When you're ready to get over it, find the good in it. Soon this will become a habit. Every problem carries with it the seed for a benefit. The only question is "How soon can you discover the benefit?"

Review

Once you have finished this, today's assignment is done. Before you move on to something else, let's review what you accomplished.

✓ You made the decision to continue the program.
✓ You read the check-in statement.
✓ You learned how your memory works.
✓ You discovered some useful memory strategies.
✓ You decided to turn failures into successes.
✓ You read your review for the day (that's this list).

 Congratulations! You have completed Day 10 of your 30 days. Close the book and we'll see you tomorrow!

Day 11

✔ **Check-in**

First, make sure you have finished the last chapter. If not, get to it ASAP. Then you can start here.

LETTING GO OF THE PAST

Why learn to let go of the past? Yesterday is a memory. Tomorrow is a hope. Today is really the only time you have to change. How you've done in the past in school means nothing. The past is *not* your potential. You can become whomever you want starting now.

To get started anew, listen to yourself think. What you think about is what or who you become. If you think about problems, you have more of them. If you think about successes, you achieve more of them. Why? Because worry is simply negative goal setting. You're simply telling your brain what you want—only you don't really want it, but your brain believes that you do, because that's the message it gets. The result? You get more of it.

First Easy Step

First, if you keep thinking of *positive* things from the past, that's great. Now begin to shift your thoughts to what you want in the future—your goals. If you think of failures and "would-of's, could-of's, and should-of's," it's time to make serious changes. It's okay to make

107

mistakes—we all do. But it's *not* okay to carry them with you every day like old baggage.

What to Do

Every time you start dwelling on something negative from the past, change your posture, stand up, sit down, lie down, start talking out loud, do anything to escape that negative frame of mind. You can pull out a pen or pencil and start writing, go for a bike ride, take ten deep breaths, listen to music, or exercise—anything that works for you. Make it a habit!

In summary, how do you let go of the past? Two ways:

1. recognize when you are recycling it
2. use the strategies mentioned above to get yourself out of those ruts

Now, think of something that bugs you from your past. It might be something you did, or wish you had done, something someone else did to you, or something you wish they had done; or it could be something that happened out of the blue.

☐ If you're willing to learn from the past and let go of it, check this box.

BETTER CONCENTRATION

You may be among the many students who complain about having poor concentration. As you know, poor

LETTING GO

concentration while studying leads to impaired attention, weak comprehension, diminished meaning, and weak recall. It certainly can adversely affect your studying speed, too. The goal of optimal concentration is to learn to identify your best state for studying. Once you've identified what it looks like, sounds like, and feels like, you have a benchmark or criteria for measurement. Once you know that you're not in the state you want to be in, you can take steps to change it. But if you never really know if you're in that optimal state, you'll never know if you need to make changes. The optimal state for studying has the following characteristics:

♦ Your body feels relaxed and posture is good.

♦ Your mind feels alert, rested, and curious.

♦ You have challenging yet achievable goals set.

♦ You have no nagging thirst or pressing hunger.

♦ You are engaged enough so that you shut out distractions.

♦ The self-talk voice in your head is positive.

♦ Nothing in the surrounding environment is annoying you.

♦ You often lose track of how much time has passed.

♦ Confidence and excitement about studying is high.

Do these conditions seem like they create a best state? Certainly! The problem is that it's easier to define the state than to make it happen. While you can learn to get into and recreate good states each time you read, those optimal states are likely to happen only now and then. The good news is that you do have a great deal of control over your particular mental, physical, and emotional states. Here are some of the things you can do to direct them to be more productive for studying.

Keep Your Eyes Healthy

Aside from the brief pauses when you blink or sleep, your eyes are working all the time. While we get help in getting our hair cut, our drains fixed, and our cars repaired, we never get training in how to take care of our eyes. No wonder so many of us suffer from eye strain or impaired vision! The three best ways to take care of the eyes are prevention, nutrition, and relaxation.

Prevention means wearing protective glasses when you are out in bright light, in dangerous areas, or using dangerous tools. Be sure you own a pair of quality sunglasses (they must screen 100 percent of UV rays). Moderate darkness provides the best protection.

Nutrition means getting plenty of vitamin A from natural food sources. It is essential for the visual process, particularly for vision in dim light or at night. The best sources of vitamin A include yellow fruits and vegetables such as carrots, squash, sweet potatoes, and corn; green leafy vegetables, dairy products, and eggs. A vitamin supplement is not enough. To be effective vitamin A must be ingested in conjunction with zinc. Both are found together in vegetables and fruit, but not necessarily in a vitamin pill.

Relaxation means learning to give the eyes breaks throughout the day. If you work at a computer, get up and walk around every 20 minutes. Look around at things that are far away (like out a window) to relax the eyes. Palming helps, too; if you wear glasses, take them off and briskly rub the palms of your hands together, creating a quick friction heat. Then, with your eyes gently closed, cup the palms of your hands lightly over your eyes—don't apply any pressure to the eyes. Hold for at least 30 seconds; you will feel gentle, soothing energy from your palms relaxing your eyes.

Avoid Dehydration

Get a drink of cool fresh water. Dehydration is a common cause of poor concentration. Often learners don't even recognize the signs because the more dehydrated you are, the less alert you are to your body's signals. You may know that the brain runs on biochemical reactions of sodium and potassium. Just like a car battery, when the water balance is low, it weakens the ability to maintain the proper electrolyte balance. As a result, connections are delayed or impaired. Before studying, you may want to have one or two glasses of water.

Stretch

The type of stretching that you see athletes do before running can be beneficial. It enhances circulation, relaxes the body, and reduces stress and tension. This can energize the mind, which is highly susceptible to stress.

Review Assignments Standing Up

Before starting to study, stand up and do a quick preview of what you haven't covered; you might also do a quick review of that which you have covered. This reorients the mind and reconnects the learning.

Close Your Eyes

This is a great way to unwind. Make sure your feet are comfortable and at least as high as the rest of your body or higher. Use low or dim lighting so that your eyes can relax fully. For three minutes, breathe in slowly through your nose and exhale slowly through your mouth. Think about pleasant thoughts. Allow your mind to wander only to things you feel are positive. At the end of the time, you'll feel rested and ready for a challenge.

Eat a Snack

Sometimes the brain runs low on energy because of low blood sugar. This condition impairs learning because one of the brain's primary fuels is glucose. It gets glucose from sugars (sucrose), fruit (fructose), or carbohydrates (it turns them into energy, too). If you plan to study for awhile, it makes sense just to have a snack or small meal. Often a large meal can cause drowsiness. Suggested snacks include the following: apple, banana, pear, orange, strawberries, a protein bar, cottage cheese, nuts, or a hard-boiled egg.

Give Yourself a Wake-Up Call

Sometimes concentration lags and you just need an increase in circulation. If so, stand up and use two hands for this one. Use one hand to rub the area just below the neck. Find with the fingers the bony area at the top of the chest and locate the little dip just below the collarbone. Gently massage that area while using the other hand to gently massage the belly button area.

After 30 seconds, switch hands. This simple exercise can help boost focus and circulation.

Get Things Off Your Mind

Sometimes you are concentrating too hard on the wrong things. Get out a piece of paper (or open up a page on your computer) and write out every concern or problem you have bugging you. Then jot down a few possible actions, steps, or solutions you can take. Keep it informal; it's more the process than the actual answers you generate. Once you've dumped the problems off your mind, it is freed to take the studying at hand.

Wake Up the Brain

If you imagine a vertical line that divides your body in half, any movement that crosses over from one side to another is going to stimulate thinking and wake up the brain. Marching is homolateral (same side), since your arms and legs usually move forward and back. You can change this into a crosslateral exercise by swinging your arms across the body, from left to right and right to left. This way, you activate the brain better. Do this for two to five minutes to attain the best benefit.

Get Ionized

The air is always electrically charged with ion particles. The more positively charged the ions are, the more stuffy it feels and the more lethargic you get. The more negatively charged the air, the more positive and exhilarated you feel. Examples of highly negatively charged environments include standing in front of a waterfall, taking a shower, being in a forest, or going outside just after a rain. When you can't do any of those, a portable ion generator, stable 75–80 percent humidity, and lots of plants can do an admirable job. If you're in a stuffy dorm room, stepping outside for some slow deep breaths of fresh air can do a great deal of good.

Change the Sounds

Concentration lags for a number of reasons. Recent research suggests the ears can be a source of energy for the brain, not just a microphone to pick up sounds. Proper frequencies can recharge and energize the brain as you have discovered when hearing an inspiring piece of music such as the Olympic fanfare or the "Hallelujah Chorus." If you are not listening to any music, you might enjoy some Mozart or Bach in the background. If you already are listening to music, and your concentration is lagging, maybe you've become too acclimated to the music. Take a break from it and put on a tape of some environmental sounds (waterfalls, birds, oceans, etc.) or simply listen to nothing. You may be pleasantly surprised by the positive effects that music can have on your studying.

Change Your Chair, the Aroma, or the Lighting

Many chairs provide poor back support, which encourages slumping, and impairs breathing. Be sure your chair is comfortable but also provides for good posture.

Recent research suggests that aromas like lemon or peppermint can mildly arouse the brain for improved attention and memory. You may want to use those in either spray, oil, or concentrates in a humidifier.

Lighting can hurt or help your studying. Studying in dim light or having a bright glare on your page can both cause eye strain and fatigue. To improve your concentration, adjust your lighting. The best is low to moderate natural lighting. The second best is moderate to bright incandescent. The worst is bright fluorescent. Do the best you can to study in the ideal lighting.

Prepare Your Mind

This mental exercise can help you prepare for studying in just a minute. You may wish to record it on tape so that you can play it back later or simply recall it and use it. Here's how it goes:

> Leave your studying materials in front of you, but closed up. Relax by closing your eyes. Increase your self-awareness from head to toe. Now your spine is erect, your posture is comfortable, your breathing is relaxed. State your goals for what you are about to read (for example, "I will successfully and quickly read this magazine article for ideas to help me improve my concentration in five minutes or less"). Become aware of yourself as relaxed and alert. Breathe in through the nose and exhale slowly through the mouth. Bring a smile to the corners of your eyes and the corners of your mouth to relax your face. Imagine your mind opening up. Feel waves of confidence moving through you. See yourself completing your

studying in less time than your goals allowed. When you are ready and it's comfortable for you, keep maintaining this state of relaxed alertness and gently open your eyes and begin studying.

Get Rid of Distractions

We often read in a cluttered room, dorm, or office. The phone is often ringing, someone in the doorway is talking, we have to hurry to make a class or meeting, and many unrelated thoughts about our lives keep entering our minds. What you want is the flow state, when you are totally absorbed in the task at hand. To do this, do your best to clear your desk, clear the distractions, put a sign on your door, or go to a quiet place to get your best studying done.

Remember, the human brain is not designed for lengthy, continuous periods of strong focus and attention. It's normal for attention to go from strong focus to a more diffused state. Learn to ride the wave when your focused concentration is at its best. When your concentration is lower, you still have some tools to use but you may simply need a ten-minute break before you can resume strong concentration.

 When you've read the preceding section, check this box. You're one step closer to your goal!

Review

Once you have finished this, today's assignment is done. Before you move on to something else, let's review what you accomplished.

✓ You made the decision to continue the program.
✓ You read the check-in statement.
✓ You learned the importance of letting go of the past.
✓ You learned strategies for handling negative self-talk.
✓ You discovered concentration strategies.
✓ You read your review for the day (that's this list).

 Congratulations! You have completed Day 11 of your 30 days. Close the book and we'll see you tomorrow!

Day 12

✔ **Check-in**

First, did you do yesterday's chapter? If not, get to it. Today we've got some truly superb strategies for those hard subjects.

TOUGH SUBJECTS: MATH, SCIENCE, AND FOREIGN LANGUAGES

If you had a master list of success secrets in each subject, it would make each one much easier, so we will create such a list. Here's what makes math a difficult subject (you'll find that some of these apply to sciences, too).

- It's rarely taught cooperatively.
- It is rarely taught using concrete tasks where you build models, hold things, find and touch angles and problems.
- It is rarely taught with real world relevance.
- It is usually taught one concept at a time, so that it's hard to get the big picture of where you're going and how it all fits together.

The good news about math is that it is slowly changing. More and more schools are using strategies that make it easier and easier to learn. But until your school adopts some of these more learner-friendly approaches to teaching it, here are some things you can do.

Keep Up with Daily Assignments

There are some subjects that you can fall behind in a bit and still catch up. That happens to almost everyone. No problem, right? Well, in math it can be deadly. Nearly every principle and example is built upon the previous one. It is one of those subjects you can't cram for. It's like learning to play a musical instrument. You cannot move on to play a harder piece until you have mastered an easier one. It is better for you to do two problems or to study for five minutes each day, than to do 20 problems each weekend. If you recognize that you are getting behind, declare a study emergency! Get help ASAP.

Get Coaching Early

To keep up with math work it helps to find a mentor (it could be almost anyone who is very good at math) for the length of the course. You might get a tutor or see your professor. Get a professor's aide or other student. Remember, even the pros (golfers, quarterbacks, track stars, and basketball players) have coaches.

Get a Study Buddy

This person has got to be one who knows the subject much better than you. The ideal situation is to make a study trade. Is there something you know well, some help you could trade in exchange for the help you're getting? If not, get a study buddy anyway. Get together with your study buddy every week, not just when you are having a tough time. If you don't understand something, ask the professor (or your mentor) *that day!*

MASTER THE TOUGH SUBJECTS

Learn the Vocabulary

Know every key word inside and out. Test yourself! If your memory is less than 100 percent, go to work. Use memory associations. Use symbols. Use colored pens and pictures. Make cartoons out of the words. Put them on flash cards. Study those words, and study them with specific examples.

Use the Power of Mental Models

Most math professors have a way of approaching math problems that is so confident that it seems automatic, but they weren't born that way. Somehow, over time, they developed a way of thinking mathematically.

Their mental model provides them with the basic framework for how they approach all math problems. It might consist of them first putting on an imaginary math hat, the thinking cap that says to them, "All problems can be solved, some are just easier than others." Then they know the magic sequence of steps to take when trying to solve a problem. They know what to try first, what to do next, and what to do if plan A fails. It's the accumulated years of math wisdom. Ask if they would put that thinking formula on paper for you—that's the model you want.

Master the Formulas

There are many ways to memorize formulas. Put them on $3'' \times 5''$ flash cards and carry them around, constantly testing yourself. Draw them, color them, and put them up on a big poster you make and hang on the wall. Learn them to music. Put on your special study tape and read a key formula; pause, then reread and pause again, letting the music fill in the pauses.

Take Super-Accurate Notes

In math, notes have to be exact, because the slightest mistake totally changes the meaning of a problem. Your notes should include the following.

- main idea or key theorem
- definitions
- examples
- rules, guidelines, tips
- all diagrams and sample problems
- professor remarks that help make things clear

Divide your note page into two columns. Keep words in the right column and examples in the left column. Spread out your information—paper is cheap! This leaves room to go back and add things later to boost comprehension.

Find the Pattern

Many times a list or page of math problems is actually one problem presented 20 different ways. What is the pattern? Ask for help. Figure out what same thing happens in each of those problems. Once you find it, you'll be able to answer many more problems successfully. Work on odd-numbered problems in your book (the ones with answers in the back), and talk your way through each one. When finished, you must know both the answer and the procedure. Talking to yourself keeps your attention and awareness high, plus it locks the learning into your memory.

Give Meaning to Theorems

Make the numbers mean something. Make up stories. Use crazy-sounding names so that you'll remember them forever.

Pretest Yourself

Do this *before* the professor tests you! Test yourself on a dozen problems without using your textbook or help of any kind. Make it a timed test. Find out what you know and don't know. Improve yourself! Make up test questions from the odd-numbered questions twice a week so you can think like the professor at test time.

When you think you are done with your homework, review several problems. Explain them out loud or to a study buddy. Your explanation is your review.

Ask These Questions

First, read the problem, reread the problem, gather information, analyze the type of problem, and sort out vocabulary or symbols. Next, ask yourself a series of questions. The answers will usually steer you in the right direction.

♦ What is this problem really asking for?

♦ How can I restate the problem?

♦ Could I use a diagram or picture to help out?

♦ Where is the backup information I need?

♦ Can I make an estimate?

♦ How will I compute this problem?

♦ Is there someone I can go to for help? (And, if I could get some kind of an answer . . .)

♦ Is my answer within reasonable boundaries?

♦ Can I prove it?

♦ Do I know both the procedure and the solution?

♦ Could I duplicate my success again and again?

Change Texts

If your book is hard to understand, get another that you can understand better. Keep your old one, but get one by another author, one that is used in another class, or one from the library. It's no shame to have difficulty in a course, the shame would be to fail a course that you could have passed.

☐ When you've read the preceding section, check this box. You're one step closer to your goal!

SCIENCE—PHYSICS, BIOLOGY, GEOLOGY . . .

In the past it was assumed that only nerds did well in science. Those days are gone. Science is not just for nerds, it's for everyone. It combines a unique mix of linear, sequential thinking with random creative thinking. It's a wonderful subject because it's as real world as you can get. The products you buy, the foods you eat, the cars you ride in all are products of science. There are many strategies that you can use to succeed in science courses. Pick the ones that you're not using now and find out what works best.

Take a Personal Field Trip

Is there a source that could better explain some theory or chapter in the textbook? How about a local science museum or exploratorium? Ask the professor for other ways to learn about the topic.

Know Where You Stand

Stay in touch with your learning. Make sure you know your terms, assignments, and scores. Do what it takes to keep up or get ahead. Get a tutor. See your professor. Get a professor's aide or other student.

There's nothing embarrassing about getting help. It's a lot better than getting a D or an F.

Find a Video or CD

There are many new shows on public television and the Discovery Channel that feature science. Some video stores even rent science videos. The media center at your school may have some videos or great material on CDs. Some of them are fun, others are more serious. They can be a great way to learn or reinforce existing learning. Get a program guide and look ahead each week to find out if there's a show that is on something you're learning. Also, you may be able to get help on the Internet. Do a search for the information you need through a browser software, like Netscape. You will find that many other students have solved the problem you're facing.

Try Things Out

You'd be surprised at how many concepts have a simple do-at-home angle to them. Ask your professor if there's something you could try out at home, in your dorm or apartment. This will not only let you do experiments at your own pace, but the work will be much more relevant. Many experiments require no money to make. They use simple items found almost anywhere. Ask your professor!

Talk to Friends

There are often several professors at your school that teach the same basic introductory courses. Do you have a friend that's in another class? If so, ask him what he's doing and learning. Another professor might make a concept simpler just by its presentation.

Professors often let their assistants run the lab portion of the class. As a result, many students use the lab as a chance to cut loose and visit with their friends. Use the experiment or lab as a source of learning. Today's professors are using the labs more and more as part of the formal grading process. Ask questions about the lab work until you understand exactly what is happening.

☐ When you've read the preceding section, check this box. You're one step closer to your goal!

FOREIGN LANGUAGES

The way you learned your native language was simple; you just picked it up from your family. You lived, ate, tried out new things, asked questions and listened, and others talked to you. In short, you immersed yourself in it. Today, years later, that's still the best way to learn a foreign language. The hardest way to learn it is by staring at a textbook. So to get the immersion effect, think of the things that worked for you as a child.

Stay Relaxed and Have Fun

As a kid, you didn't work at learning your native language. Threats and pressure can inhibit learning. Keep your stress down, do silly things, learn games with your new language. If you need to, do a short relaxation and breathing exercise to get your mind and body ready to learn.

Make Up a Colorful Language Map

On a 2′ × 3′ piece of paper, write out the key words you need to learn. Arrange them either in the form of a clock, spokes of a wheel, or a story that winds around the page. Draw colorful picture clues. Hang the language map on your wall. Just keeping it around will help your brain make the right associations. For example:

I stood on a *box* and used *el mano* to dial the *telefono*. Los numeros fue *tres, tres, uno, dos, cinco, tres,* y *cuatro*.

Or: My *diente* hurt, so I rode my *bicicleta* to the dentist. On the way, I saw a young *perro,* heard *musica,* thought of my *novia,* decided to get *flores* for her, and remembered *el futbol* on Saturday night.

Listen to Language Tapes Three Times

Many times, students listen to a language tape once, then get discouraged because they didn't really get it. However, you never approached your native language that way. You heard words, phrases, and sentences around the house hundreds of times before they became part of your natural expression. Plan on listening to a foreign language tape at least three separate times.

First, listen just to get used to the tempo, tone, and pitch. It's a casual listen; you can even do something else while you listen. Second, listen while you follow along in the text. The third time, relax and listen with your eyes closed. This lets your brain really absorb it. The college library or media center often has language tapes to listen to or check out and take home.

You might also put on the language tapes and leave them on while you do other things. The first time I planned a trip to Denmark, I listened to commercially available Danish tapes for weeks before I went. Before I understood a word, I got very comfortable with the tone, speed, pitch, pauses, and words. That way, when I began to learn the language, I already had a feel for it.

Involve Yourself in Real Conversation

Nothing beats the real thing: listening to others who speak the language. If you can, visit an area where that language is spoken. In some large and diverse cities, many people still speak their native language. Are there language clubs on campus? Find out and join them. Find study partners who will practice conversing with you.

Start with the Familiar

Discover as many words in the foreign language as you can that look or sound like their English counterparts. European languages, especially German, Spanish, French, and Italian, often have a large number of familiar words. First things first: find out what you already know. Make a list or create flash cards. Reviewing them boosts vocabulary and confidence.

Keep Up with the Class

You might have to let work for another course slip for a few days or even a week, but not a language class. You can't cram for language. Learning it depends on what you already know. Stay with it. Do something in it every day if you can. Make sure you have the vocabulary and verbs and are comfortable at each level.

Make the Language Natural

Remember the principle of immersion? The more visual and auditory cues that you give your brain, the more likely you'll learn to think in that language. Get books in the language, souvenirs and flags from a country where the language is spoken. Put up posters and scenery from that country. Go to restaurants where that kind of food is served and learn to read the menu (if it's in that language).

Find a Study Partner

Is there someone in your class (or a friend outside the class) that is a native speaker in that language? They'd obviously know the subject much better than you. The ideal situation is to make a study trade. Is there something you know well, some help you could trade in exchange for the help you're getting? If not, get a study buddy anyway. Get together with your study buddy every week, not just when you are having a tough time. The study buddy not only gives you a reality check on what you know and don't know, but provides much needed support.

When you've read the preceding section, check this box. You're one step closer to your goal!

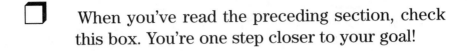

Review

Once you have finished this, today's assignment is done. But before you celebrate, let's review what you accomplished.

✓ You made the decision to continue the program.
✓ You read the check-in statement.
✓ You discovered great math strategies.
✓ You learned solid science grade boosters.
✓ You were introduced to foreign language tips.
✓ You read your review for the day (that's this list).

 Congratulations! You have completed Day 12 of your 30 days. Close the book and we'll see you tomorrow!

Day 13

 Check-in

First, did you complete yesterday's chapter?
If not, get to it as soon as you can, before you
begin today. Then you can start here.

REVIEW AND PREVIEW

Remember Day 6, when we did a photoflash sneak preview of the whole book? It gives your brain sneak previews well in advance. It plants seeds for future learning and makes each day have more meaning when you do get to it. And instead of trying to recall everything you've learned, every single day, we'll do simple weekly reviews. The more times we do this, the more the material becomes natural to you.

PHOTOFLASH

In case you don't remember how to do the photoflash preview, here's a quick review. Simply take a look at each page for the shortest length of time you can, like a photoflash! Let your brain absorb as much or as little as naturally happens in that time. Turn the page, glance at it for one second or less, then look at the next page. Use a relaxed, soft focus with your eyes, purposely not trying to read anything. Just glance at it as you would a picture. At one second per page, this entire book (all 30 chapters) will go very quickly.

You'll continue doing this on each of the next two photoflash days. By the end of the course, this same exercise becomes a powerful review. And it will take very little time, too. Go ahead and photoflash every page in this book. That's all you will do today. Turn pages and glance at them.

☐ When you're through, check this box.

Review

Once you have finished this, today's assignment is done. Before you close the book and move on to something else, let's review what you accomplished:

✓ You made the decision to continue the program.
✓ You read the check-in statement.
✓ You photoflashed the whole 30-day program.
✓ You read your review for the day (that's this list).

 Congratulations! You have completed Day 13 of your 30 days. Close the book and we'll see you tomorrow!

Day 14

FREE DAY

Today is a free-to-be-me day. It means you can do whatever you feel like doing. Go to the beach (or create your own beach), hang out with friends, rent a B movie and make fun of it, visit long-lost relatives, pursue a hobby, call your family, or just relax (probably not at the same time, though). You are allowed to study if you choose to, but why not just take a break today? Have some fun!

Review

Once you have finished this, today's assignment is over. Before you close the book and move on to something else, let's review what you accomplished.

✓ You made the decision to continue the program.
✓ You read the check-in statement.
✓ You figured out what you want to do for fun today.
✓ You read your review for the day (that's this list).

 Congratulations! You have completed Day 14 of your 30 days. Close the book and we'll see you tomorrow!

Day 15

 Check-in
Are you finished with yesterday? If not, get to
it. Then start here.

MEGA-MOTIVATION AND MOMENTUM

Motivation is fairly easy, once you learn how it
works. You are already good at motivating yourself to
do the things you like. No problem. Now you want to
become good at motivating yourself to do other things.
Believe it or not, things like studying and assignments
can become much easier to do once you have learned
how to motivate yourself.

You might have discovered that there are those who
are consistently, positively, massively motivated. How
do they do it? The truth is that there is no one single
motivating secret. If there was, we'd all be super motivated every day. Every person has to discover, through
trial and error, what things motivate him or her. This
chapter gives you a menu from which to select from 20
strategies.

The best way to use this chapter is to browse
through it first. For any idea or strategy that you like
and have already used, put a check or a star next to it.
You'll want to use it again if it worked for you. If you are
unsure if you like the idea, put a question mark next
to it. If you really like the idea and are willing to try it,
put some other indicator next to it, so you can find it

quickly later on. Try each idea; that's how you'll learn what works best to motivate you. Let's get started with the first strategy.

Motivate Your Brain with Positives (Benefits)

Give your brain a strong positive association with studying. Think of (or pick from) these positive benefits of studying smart.

- less worrying
- better grades
- more pride in yourself
- more self-discipline
- making it in athletics

And since your good grades will keep you in school, you can also make a lot of money! Did you know that the average high school dropout earns about $250,000 in a lifetime? College graduates are said to earn well over a million dollars in their lifetime.

Key Point

You are always more motivated to do something that you absolutely *must* do than something that someone else thinks you *ought* to do.

Make up three strong reasons why you *must* do well in school:

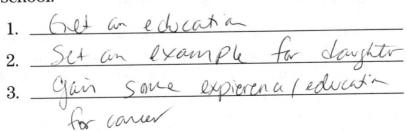

1. _Get an education_
2. _Set an example for daughter_
3. _Gain some experience / education for career_

Motivate Your Brain with Negatives (Bad Effects)

You don't like pain. Use that to your advantage! Think of the painful results of not studying:

- no good jobs
- your parents will go nuts
- no college or university degree
- no decent money
- low confidence and low self-esteem
- loss of pride

And that's not all.

- You might drop out of school.
- Your friends might think you're stupid.
- You won't be able to attract a quality boyfriend or girlfriend.
- You'll feel like a failure.
- You will have wasted your time on this program!

Now it's your turn. Write out the three worst things that could happen if you don't study or get good grades:

1. _No Career_
2. _bad example_
3. _failure_

Ask Others What Works for Them

When you're around others, find out what motivates them. Ask questions. "How did you know to try that idea?" Or "Why are you trying to get an A in that class?" You'd be surprised how many others have figured out solutions to problems that you're still working on.

What else is good for motivating you? Here are another 17 ideas. Even if one sounds a bit weird, it may be the one that will work the best. After all, you've already tried many of the strategies that sound obvious or are guaranteed to work. Which one of these could you use?

Review Your Short and Long-Term Goals

What's this? You don't have short or long-term goals? They are great for motivation. They focus the mind and give you something to strive for.

Example: My short-term goal is, in the next 30 days, to get an A or B on something. My long-term goal is to graduate with at least a 3.0 average so I can feel proud, prove to myself I'm smart, and have more career choices.

Now it's your turn: Stop and set some goals. Write two of them here:

Short-term goal: *Get an A in this Class*

Long-term goal: *finish certificate requirements*

My promise to myself is: I will read my goals every single day for the next 30 days.

Visualize Success

Every thought you think forms a habit, even if it's just a mental habit. Worry often enough and you'll get good at worrying. Purposely visualize success, the way Olympic athletes do. It will increase your chances of success.

VISUALIZE SUCCESS

Example: Instead of worrying about getting poor grades, visualize yourself studying successfully and often. Then visualize yourself getting a good grade report and being very happy about it.

Now it's your turn: Stop right now. Do you worry a lot? A little is OK. But if you worry a lot, you are simply practicing stress and failure.

My promise to myself is: Each time I start worrying about failing, I'll pause and make sure I visualize succeeding instead.

Put on Motivating Music

Everybody has some songs that motivate them. What songs do it for you? Are they rap, rock, jazz, or classical?

Example: One favorite is the theme from *Raiders of the Lost Ark.*

Now it's your turn: Think of a song that really gets you going. If none comes to mind, be patient. You'll discover one that does.

My promise to myself is: The next time I hear or think of a great motivating piece of music, I'll write it down. Then I'll find a way to get a recording of it so I can play it when I need it.

Make a Bet with Someone

Are you the type of person who gets a lot of satisfaction from doing something that others say you couldn't do? Make a bet with someone about something you'll do that she doesn't think you can do.

Example: Can you get a better grade on a test? Can you turn in a paper on time? Can you get a passing grade or a high mark in a course? Can you make the dean's list?

Now it's your turn: Find the person you will make this bet with. Figure out an item to bet on, like frozen yogurt, pizza, or a personal favor. Write the bet down on paper to make it official.

My promise to myself is: I'll find that person this week and make a bet.

Read Your Posted Affirmations

What is an affirmation poster? It's a simple printed reminder that keeps you motivated. You've seen such posters with positive sayings on them in college or pro locker rooms. Why not have your own? Make them on your computer or on 3″ × 5″ cards. Use colored pens and make borders or simple illustrations. The whole point of this is to keep the intensity and drive alive.

Examples:
- Yard by Yard, It's Hard—But Inch by Inch, It's a Cinch
- If It Can Be Done, I Can Do It
- Everything Worthwhile Takes Effort
- Don't Sweat the Small Stuff
- If I Can Dream It, I Can Do It
- Do It!

Now it's your turn: Start noticing other motivational posters or sayings you like. You can also make up your own. Write them down or just save them in your brain. Once you've settled on a few, it's time to put them into action.

My promise to myself is: Within the next seven days, I will figure out and create at least three motivational affirmation cards or posters.

Pretend You Are Motivated

You might wonder how all those pumped up motivational speakers like Tony Robbins get psyched up every day. The answer is that they don't always feel motivated. But they know that it's easier *to act your way into feeling than to feel your way into acting.* Don't wait until you feel like doing something, just go ahead and do it.

Example: Let's say you don't feel like going to a certain class. But once you're there and you start participating, it's not so bad. Pretty soon, you've forgotten what it was that turned you off about class. By *acting* interested, you actually *got* interested.

Now it's your turn: Think of something that you dread doing so much that you put it off or, worse you just don't do it. Now, ask yourself, "How would I go about doing this if I was fully motivated to do it now?"

My promise to myself is: The next time I feel lethargic and unmotivated, I'll try out this tool. I'll act as if I'm motivated and see what happens.

Break Up the Work into Small Segments of Two to Five Minutes Each

If a part of a big task is small enough, it's often easier to get motivated to do it. A journey of a thousand miles begins with a single step.

Example: Many times you don't feel like reading a book or even a chapter, but you can get yourself motivated to read three pages. Then decide to read another three pages. Maybe you'll end up reading a whole chapter, maybe not. It's worth a try.

Now it's your turn: Practice breaking up big tasks into smaller ones.

My promise to myself is: The next time I feel overwhelmed by a task, I'll stop. Instead of getting all negative about it, I'll ask myself, What's the smallest part of this that I can do quickly and easily?

Eat Smart

The latest brain research suggests that what we eat can dramatically affect our moods. Why eat smart? Your brain comprises only 2–5 percent of your total body weight, but it consumes 20–25 percent of your body's oxygen energy. If you feed your brain well, you'll be able to think more clearly, study at more flexible hours, and accomplish more in less time. Certain foods have been proven to be better for the brain because they provide essential amino acids for thinking and memory.

I LIKE CRAMMING FOR AN EXAM

Dr. Judith Wurtman and Dr. Keith Connors recommend the following.

First Easy Step

Improve eating habits and work out three to six times a week.

1. Eat more
   - fruits: all are good, apples and bananas especially.
   - vegetables: most are good; broccoli is great, the darker the vegetable, the better.
   - pasta, brown rice, and wheat germ.
   - eggs, yogurt, nuts, peanut butter.
   - vitamin and mineral supplements.
   - pure water (six to eight glasses a day) and fruit juices (less soft drinks).
2. Eat less
   - fatty foods (deep fat fried, greasy).
   - dry snacks (potato chips, crackers, cookies, cake, pastry, candy bars); have them after 3 P.M. if you do eat them.
   - dairy products (they clog your system).
3. Timing is everything!
   - Eat your proteins first at breakfast and lunch—it improves thinking and memory.
   - Have fruits and salads early in the day.
   - After school, have the carbohydrates.
4. Work out three to six times a week! Your body is yours 24 hours a day, seven days a week. Take care of it! More than anything else, to keep your brain happy, it needs oxygen. It gets oxygen from

foods high in water content like fruits, vegetables, and pasta. And it gets oxygen from your breathing. The more and deeper you breathe, the happier your brain is.

Working out forces more oxygen into the lungs. It keeps the body healthy and helps keep you from getting sick. Do something vigorous, three to six times a week for at least 20 minutes at a time.

♦ Play a sport.

♦ Ride a bike, walk, or swim.

♦ Go to a gym and work out.

When you've read the preceding section, check this box. You're one step closer to your goal!

Redefine the Task

Two stonecutters were working in a courtyard. The first one was constantly complaining and unhappy. The second one worked with a song in his heart and a smile on his face. A visitor asked the first one what he was doing. He said, "I'm cutting these stupid stones." Then the visitor asked the second stonecutter what he was doing. He beamed and said, "I'm building a beautiful cathedral." Same job, two different attitudes.

Example: The next time, instead of saying, "I have this stupid math class to go to," say, "I'm getting an education." Instead of having a "stupid paper to write," tell yourself, "I'm building my career skills."

Now it's your turn: Figure out ahead of time what you'll say to yourself (I wouldn't say it out loud to your friends) the next time your motivation drops. Remember the two stonecutters and what a difference your attitude makes.

My promise to myself is: I will learn to think of the long-term goal to stay motivated and I will change my attitude to gain motivation.

Start with Something Easy or Enjoyable

Nearly every task has dozens of minor tasks that are part of the larger one. Some of the smaller tasks are easy and some are fun. There may even be some that are both. That's a good place to start.

Example: Let's say you've got a research paper to write. What's the easiest place to start? Is it getting your working area put together? Is it figuring out a topic? Is it doing some research? You be the judge!

Now it's your turn: Start thinking about the tasks that you have trouble motivating yourself to do. In your mind, before you encounter those tasks again, have your first steps already worked out.

My promise to myself is: The next time I feel stuck and unmotivated, I'll find the easiest and most fun place to start.

Change Your Mental or Physical State

All of our decisions, beliefs, and actions are filtered through our own mind and body. If you are scared, every sound can send chills up your spine. If you're in love, you're unaffected by minor bad news.

Example: When you're all cozy and bundled up, you rarely feel like going out on a cold night to do laundry, get Chinese food or pizza. But when you're already out, driving or walking around, adding a new errand to an existing one is fairly painless. In other words, do something similar to (but different from) what you're avoiding.

Now it's your turn: The next time you don't feel like studying, change your mental and physical state. Get up, get a drink of water, go outside for a minute, stretch or put on some music. Anything to get out of the funk you're in.

My promise to myself is: No more complaining about studying. If I don't feel like doing it, I'll change my state of mind so that I do.

Draw Upon Past Successes

There is always some kind of extreme sport that's popular. They've included snow boarding, sky diving, big wave surfing, fire walking, bungee jumping, rock climbing, or motocross. Often someone who has done one of these sports says to herself, "If I've done this, I could do almost anything!" The confidence from one area of life can give you the courage to try things in other areas.

Example: If you've ever said something romantic or written poetry for yourself or a friend, you could write it for a class. If you've ever researched something for your computer or a trip you want to take, you can research a paper.

Now it's your turn: The next time you wonder if you can do something, pause. Think of what the skill is or what qualities it requires. You may be surprised that you already have done what's needed, but in another form. You just hadn't thought of it that way.

My promise to myself is: I'll realize that I have probably done part or all of everything that others ask of me. It's just a matter of putting the pieces together and using it in the right way.

Think of What You'll Do After You Get It Done

If you don't like where you're at right now, use your imagination to put yourself into the past (find a pleasant experience) or the future (what you'll do when you're done).

Example: Let's say it's hard getting into writing an English paper. Pause for a moment and think about all the things you could do (that are much more fun) when you're done (like browse the Net, call a friend, read a favorite book, watch a favorite TV show, or get some sleep).

Now it's your turn: Make yourself a promise to avoid getting "negged out" (that's when you get really negative about something) over something you can deal with now.

My promise to myself is: The next time I start to get negged out, I'll switch mindsets and go for the future positive one.

Make a Better Environment

We all know that environments make a difference in our motivation. It could be the people, the color on the walls, the noise, the posters, the plants, or the lack of any of those. In the right environment, you're much more likely to be motivated. But you have to know what that right environment is and take action.

Example: Some students find that bright colors keep them psyched up. What colors are around you when you study? Scientists have found that light blue, green, yellow, and gray are good for learning.

Now it's your turn: The next time you are in an environment that you find motivating, in school or out, take notice. You might even make a list on paper of what you think makes that a good learning environment.

My promise to myself is: I will learn from those good environments I find and implement items from those into my own study area.

Hang Around Motivating People

A culture is really about the people of any area, land, or country. The people you hang around with create a mini-culture that's either positively motivated, neutral, or unmotivated.

Example: With some friends, you're more likely to get out and do active stuff. With others, you're more likely to just hang out and do nothing.

Now it's your turn: Have you ever noticed what the impact of others is on your motivation levels? It's time to do that now. If the news is bad, change it. If it's good, congratulate yourself and work on other areas of motivation.

My promise to myself is: Once I've discovered who my most motivated friends are, I'll hang around them more often and spend less time around the others.

Change What You Believe

If you believe the task is hard or that you can't do it easily or that you'll do a poor job, you'll avoid it. After all who wants pain?

Example: You might put off doing a research paper because you don't know an easy way (yet) to do it or a smart way to get a high grade on it (yet).

Now it's your turn: Start identifying those moments when you say to yourself, "I don't want to do this." Now, ask yourself, "Why?" If you were assured that you'd get it done quickly and get a high grade on it would you be more motivated? If so, that's your clue. It's your belief that is getting in the way.

My promise to myself is: The next time I feel like avoiding or procrastinating, I'll stop and rethink what I really believe about getting it done. By changing my beliefs, I can motivate myself better.

Give Yourself More Feedback

One of the most motivating things for the human brain is constant feedback. The feedback gives you either (1) the information you need to make changes in what you do or (2) the confirmation that you're on the right track. Many of the most motivated people use simple daily checklists.

Example: Video games have a huge amount of built-in feedback. The player always knows where he is. Computers give you feedback at every moment. If you press the wrong key, it lets you know. In school, quizzes and tests are a form of feedback, but they can be too vague, too little, or too late. You need something better.

Now it's your turn: Make out a list of small tasks for every day. As you complete your checklist, cross out each item. Make a list of weekly goals. Create a list of more long-term goals. Keep adjusting, keep checking them off. Give yourself feedback on how you're doing.

My promise to myself is: I'll start up some kind of list in the next 24 hours and begin to use it daily.

Well, now you have it. A list of the 20 most motivating strategies you'll find anywhere. You may have noticed that I left off the list gimmicks, bribes, and rewards. Certainly there may be a place for them, but for now, let's concentrate on building motivation from within. That way, it'll be longer lasting and more satisfying. Now that you've checked out this list, have you figured out which of the items you'll start using? If not, that's the next step. Go ahead, motivate yourself now.

☐ When you've read the section above, check this box. You're one step closer to your goal!

Review

Once you have absorbed this chapter, think about the motivational strategies you can use. Before you close the book and move on to something else, let's review what you accomplished.

✓ You made the decision to continue the program.
✓ You read the check-in statement.
✓ You learned a truckload of motivating strategies.
✓ You discovered what and how to eat better.
✓ You figured out which ones you'll use.
✓ You read your review for the day (that's this list).

 Congratulations! You have completed Day 15 of your 30 days. That's the halfway mark. Close the book and we'll see you tomorrow!

Day 16

 Check-in

First, did you complete yesterday's chapter?
If not, get to it now. Today will be a full day!

LOCATE RESOURCES

How do you locate the best resources? That's what this section is all about. It takes a lot to get B's and A's in just 30 days. Sometimes you'll need help. But do you know where to get help? Learn to develop a team that will help you reach your goals. Your team players will be the people, places, and things that will give you the power to get higher grades.

First Easy Step

On the list below, fill in both the people (friends, tutors, professors, aides) and resources (computer, books, library, phone).

Course: _____ Resources: _____

_____

Course: _____ Resources: _____

_____

Course: _____ Resources: _____

_____

Course: _____ Resources: _____

_____

Course: _____ Resources: _____

_____

Are any categories left blank? Today, right now, start figuring out how and where you can get help in those areas. Where else can you find information? The possibilities are limitless.

➤ on-line databases through providers like Compu-Serve or America Online (AOL)

➤ Newsearch, a database from over 3,000 publications

➤ newsletters; consult *Newsletters In Print* in the library

➤ borrow, purchase, or use CD-ROMs from a media center

➤ *World Book, Collier's,* or *Encyclopedia Britannica*

➤ public libraries, public interlibrary reference loans

➤ interlibrary computer connections

➤ your friends, relatives, their parents, and community members

➤ university and college libraries

➤ museum or exhibit libraries

➤ magazine articles; use the *Guide to Periodical Literature*

➤ newspaper articles; use *National Newspaper Index*

➤ *Facts on File* or *The New York Times* On-line Database

➤ Almanacs; *The World Almanac and Book of Facts* and *The Information Please Almanac*

➤ dictionaries; many offer you more than definitions

➤ Who's Who publications, like *Who's Who in America*

➤ U.S. Government publications

DEAL WITH DISTRACTIONS

What happens when your motivation to get better grades conflicts with distractions, such as friends, TV shows, or a professor you don't like? Learn to deal with it! Time, effort, and determination are required to get what you want. Learn to deal with the distractions, and you'll have an edge over those who can't.

Here's how to deal with the three biggest distractions to motivation.

Challenge 1:

You're doing homework. A friend calls and wants to get some food or hang out for awhile. You want to stick to your B's and A's program, so you say: "Thanks for asking, but I *have* to study tonight. Maybe next time, OK? Thanks!"

If your friends are persistent, you be more persistent. Keep saying the same thing until they get the message.

Challenge 2:

You're supposed to be doing homework, but you dislike the class, dislike the professor, and don't feel like going on any longer. Try any of these.

DEALING WITH DISTRACTIONS

- ◆ Study micro-small parts just to get going.
- ◆ Take a one-minute walk-around, psych-up break.
- ◆ Think about how good it will feel to finish the home-work.
- ◆ Figure out ways to make the class more interesting.

Challenge 3:

You've got a big test tomorrow, and there's an awe-some movie on TV. You can

- ◆ tape the show and watch it later.
- ◆ set a date to rent it from the video store.

♦ jump into your studying and get so much done that you finish up with time to watch the second half. Review your notes during commercials!

☐ When you've read the preceding section, check this box. You're one step closer to your goal!

USE THE POWER OF RAPPORT

Rapport means affinity, harmony, or being in tune with another. It means you're on the same wavelength, things are clicking, and you both feel good about each other. When there is rapport between two people, communication is easy and automatic. When there's not, it's drudgery.

Think about this: you get grades from people, and there are lots of intangible things that affect your grade. If a professor likes you, you're more likely to be thought of favorably, whether the professor means to do it or not. It may or may not affect your grade. What's certain is that it never hurts to have a professor think of you favorably, especially if you're on the border between a C and a B or a B and an A.

You need to maintain rapport with others—especially your professors. It's possible to do it, even if you don't like the professor. Here's how: simply demonstrate an understanding and appreciation of their world. You can disagree without being disagreeable. When a professor is talking to you, never react with the word *but*. Instead, say something like, "I appreciate that . . . and here's how I came to a different conclusion."

Basically, rapport means being willing to walk in their shoes—it's tuning in and operating on the same wavelength. Rapport is powerful and it works.

First Easy Step

Build academic relationships with your professors. It makes you more accessible to ask questions, gather information, and take the course more intelligently. This may mean just two minutes once a week, but it will all add up. Give it a try.

Review

Once you have finished this, today's assignment is done. Before you close this book and move on to something else, let's review what you accomplished.

✓ You made the decision to continue the program.
✓ You read the check-in statement.
✓ You learned where to locate resources.
✓ You were reminded of how to deal with distractions.
✓ You discovered the power of rapport.
✓ You read your review for the day (that's this list).

 Congratulations! You have completed Day 16 of your 30 days. You're past the halfway mark. Close the book and we'll see you tomorrow!

Day 17

KEEP YOUR SELF-ESTEEM SKY HIGH

Self-esteem is not how you feel about yourself. Feelings go up and down every day. Self-esteem is the relationship between your values and your life. If you value being honest and you live your life honestly, that will contribute to your self-esteem. However if you steal and cheat, you'll not only feel guilty, you'll also feel like a miserable person, because you have to cheat to survive.

Why worry about self-esteem? To get top grades, you've got to believe in yourself every single day. You'll get the grades you think you deserve. If you think you deserve a lot, you'll be more likely to get B's and A's.

First Easy Step

First, let's find out what is good about you. Complete the following questions:

1. I know my best friends think I'm _____

   _____

2. I am unique and different because _____

   _____

3. What I do best is _____

   _____

4. I know I'm a good person because _____

   _____

5. More people would like me better if they knew that_____

   _____

6. The best way for me to demonstrate that quality is _____

   _____

Next, think of a mistake you made recently. Then think of professions where people make lots of mistakes. Basketball players may miss half of all their shots; baseball players miss two-thirds and more of all pitched balls. If they practice their profession every day, all day and *still* make mistakes, maybe mistakes are OK.

You can make all the mistakes in the world, and it's okay if you remember just three things about mistakes.

1. Never hide them or try to cover them up. Everyone makes them, but only a few are honest enough to admit it.
2. Learn from them—you can grow and become better because of each mistake. Stop and reflect each time you mess up. What did I do? What could I do different next time?
3. Remember that you are still a good person, even when you make mistakes. You are not your mistakes.

☐ If you understand these three things, check this box.

MAKING CHOICES

Everyday you make dozens or even hundreds of choices. It's time to make another decision. Do you want to conquer getting better grades once and for all? Would you like to eliminate nasty, slow-study learning habits permanently? You can. But you have to *decide* to do that. It won't just happen automatically. This is a choice you'll have to make over and over until it becomes a habit. At that point, it happens automatically.

Make the choice to use these tools, and you will find it within your power to make your best-case study and learning scenario come true for you. However, making a new path means more than trying new study and learning behaviors. You'll want to adopt a whole new and wider view of what study and learning can be.

Your old way worked when you had very little to study and learn. The old model of study and learning is passive, stuffy, hard, frustrating, and yields little. You often felt pressure to get it right the first time with your old way of study and learning. You expect to comprehend everything in one pass through the material. Otherwise, you feel inadequate as a studier and a learner. What kind of a system is that? It just doesn't make sense in this fast-paced world where information is the currency of our lives. There is another way, but you have to choose it. It's the path outlined in this book. Here are three suggestions for you.

Make the Choice to Start Now

Instead of choosing to think it over, just start anywhere. When it comes to better study skills, it's best to go cold turkey. Just jump in and make it happen. You can start at any time, on any material, with any skill level. Avoid waiting until you have perfected the skills in this 30-day book. They'll always be in the process of getting better.

What is one positive new choice you can make now?

_____

For example, implement one secret to great recall from Day 10.

☐   Check this box when you have made your choice.

Choose to Think Positive

Give up any negative thoughts or voices in your head about being a poor learner. You'll recall the student who said, "I just don't think I am cut out to learn this. And if I did study and learn fast, I wouldn't get it. And if I get it, I wouldn't enjoy it. And if I enjoy it, I wouldn't recall it. And if I recall it, my skills wouldn't last." That's an example of a pattern that will cause failure.

Here's another way to go. Another student said, "I am going to learn this, one way or another. If I get stuck, I'll find another way. If I don't do well, I'll study the book and find out where I went wrong. If my skills are weak, I'll practice more. In fact, I'll do whatever it takes to master this."

Both of the students above actually have the ability to do well. The latter student in our example found it easy to learn and mastered the skills more quickly. The first student found it much more difficult to discover the true abilities she possessed as a learner. The difference? You have to choose to be better, not just hope it happens.

What is one negative thought you can turn into a positive? _____ negative _____ positive

⬜ When you have done this, check box on left.

Choose the Movies in Your Mind

Your thoughts are powerful. Every thought you think makes the likelihood of thinking that thought again even higher. Be careful what you say and what you think or dream. That affects your future! Let's begin the practice in our mind. Here's the best way to direct your mental movies.

Take a moment to paint a vivid mental picture of the kind of study and learning success you want. Begin succeeding in your mind, for a few moments. See it, hear it, and feel it. Whenever a negative or failure thought comes into your mind, just say to yourself, "There goes one of those negative thoughts. Fortunately, since I created it, I can also make it go away."

Then, once again, begin to choose positive thoughts. Whenever you study and learn, choose to do so with a sense of effortlessness and relaxation. Choose to make your conversation and writing articulate, fluid, and persuasive. Choose to finish your study and learning tasks with time to spare. Choose to absorb several books in the time it used to take you to study and learn just one.

Now, choose to expand your positive expectancy to other areas of your life. Create the future you want in health, in your relationships, in entertainment, and in sports, family, and your hobbies. Keep this future in your mind for a few more seconds. Savor the resulting feelings of pleasure. Remember now, those feelings of success are all of your own making. You choose to be successful. That's what life is all about—making smart choices. Start today by making one new smart choice. Make it again and it's a habit. Make it often enough and it becomes your character. Make it for a lifetime and it becomes your legacy.

If you're not going to visualize success now, when do you plan to do it? Day of week_____

time of day_____

☐   Check this box when you have made your decision.

BUILDING SELF-CONFIDENCE

Is there a single secret to building self-confidence? No, but there are many things you can do that will, in time, dramatically raise the self-confidence of any learner. How do you know which ones to do? Explore! Every activity has its own limitations and possibilities. Some of these can be done in class, others by yourself while working, and some might be homework assignments for youngsters.

Give Up the Myths

- the myth that you are dependent on others for happiness
- the myth that change takes years and is painful and horrible
- the myth that you can only do what others say you can
- the myth that you are less than a good and powerful person
- the myth that to get ahead you have to cheat, steal, manipulate, or inherit
- the myth that you are not good enough to totally succeed in anything you

What one myth about yourself are you determined to change? _____

_____

☐   Jot it down now, then check the box on the left.

Know Yourself

Recognize your own learning styles, personality styles, multiple intelligences, and stress habits. Know your strengths and weaknesses. The more you know about yourself, the more comfortable you can be with yourself and the more realistic you can be about your ability to accomplish new things.

What new strength have you learned you possess?

☐ Fill it in now, then check the box on left.

Develop a Purpose in Life

Having a purpose gives clarity to your life. And clarity gives you power to act on your dreams. Think about your purpose. Figure out, develop, explore, and decide what you want to accomplish in your life. Take the time for personal introspection. Take time to be sure that it is something you really want to do. It will bring self-confidence. For example:

> For the first 25 years of my life, I just wanted to have fun, make money and be liked. During my late 20s I set out to develop a real sense of why I am here and what I wanted to do with my life. My own purpose is to discover my own gifts and share them with the world. My mission is to make a positive, significant, and lasting impact on the way the world learns.

What do you think your purpose might be?

☐ Brainstorm and write down a few ideas. Then check the box on left.

Develop an Expertise

No one expects you to be good at everything, but others do sometimes ask much of you. One way to build self-confidence is to learn to become an expert in something. If you take it on as a special project, you can literally become a knowledgeable expert in just 12 months. That means doing research, attending conferences and workshops, talking to others, reading books, and developing a serious point of view about a topic.

In order for you to feel confident, you need to know what you are good at and then make sure that you do it—either for a living or recreationally. But in either case, do it often.

What is one area in which you would *like* to be an

expert? _____

What's the first step you can take? _____

When will you start? _____

☐ Check this box when you have decided.

Take Risks

There's a big difference between being careless, reckless, or out of control and taking calculated risks. Taking smart risks allows you to stretch your boundaries of skill and confidence. That gives you a chance to grow, to learn new things, and to discover strengths you may not have known you had. If you fail at something you tried to do, at least you can say, "I gave it my best shot." But if you don't even try, you'll always wonder, "Could I have done that? Could I have succeeded? Who could I have become?" Here are a few suggestions for the kinds of appropriate risks you can take.

- risk meeting new people
- risk rejection from someone
- risk failing at something
- risk learning a new skill
- risk telling the truth
- risk being intimate
- risk saying no
- risk learning a new language
- risk admitting a mistake
- risk committing to a task
- risk outgrowing old habits
- risk stating your vision
- risk setting high goals
- risk unconditional loving
- risk being happy
- risk eating a new food
- risk setting higher standards
- risk being foolish
- risk wearing new styles
- risk laughing out loud
- risk writing a book

Be adventurous and take one new risk today. What will it be? _____

☐ Write your risk here and check the box on left.

Read Success Stories

There are hundreds, maybe thousands, of stories about ordinary people who put themselves in extraordinary circumstances. As a result they were forced to either grow or die. And of course, they grew. Reading inspiring stories is a great way to understand the real thought processes of having self-confidence. Examples of powerful stories include *The Power of One* and *Atlas Shrugged*.

Think of a success story you've read recently. Why did it inspire you? _____

How might this inspirational story impact or change your life? _____

☐   Write your ideas and then check the box on left.

Be Selective About Media

There are many shows or movies that bring out the best in us. There are also those that don't. Most of the great musicals like *Les Miserables*, *West Side Story*, and *The Sound of Music* can evoke self-confidence. On television, watch shows that demonstrate the best in people. There are always positive messages in *Dr. Quinn, Medicine Woman* as well as in *MacGyver*, the man who does good in the world without ever using a gun to do it. Watch movies that emphasize building relationships and growing and achievement instead of winning at the expense of others.

If you were exposed to any media today, what positive or negative message went into your brain?

_____

☐   Write what you learned, and check box on left.

Use Affirmations

Everyone needs an occasional boost. Positive affirmations can come in many forms. One recommended product known as I Can consists of 101 affirmation cards in a can. Order from GBE publishers at (206) 454-0724. You may also order success booklets and posters from a company called Successories. Get that catalog by calling (800) 535-2773. Keep positive reminders all around, in books, in organizers, on the refrigerator, and in the bathroom.

Create one positive affirmation about yourself and

stick it an obvious place. Begin with "I am _____

_____ ."

☐   When done, check box on left.

Learn to Shape Your World

All of us are out of touch with reality. That's because we never get a chance to experience it. We all have strong filters that delete and distort most of the sensory information coming into our brains. If we were aware of everything we experienced, we would be so flooded, overwhelmed, and deluged with data, we would have to be locked up in a nuthouse within an hour. Instead, we experience a small portion of the sights, sounds, feelings, tastes, and smells of the world.

Everything that happens to you can be categorized, understood, and remembered as either positive, neutral, or negative. It can be stored in your brain as a boost to your self-confidence, as neutral, or damaging to your confidence. Which category will you store the events in? It's up to you. When you fail do you conclude that you are incompetent, worthless, and unlovable? Or do you say that you had a *less-than* moment? Those are the moments in which you were *less than* your best self. We all have those.

The difference between successes and failures is not how many times you are knocked to the ground, but how many times you get up and try again with a new strategy. Shape your internal world with conclusions that you are capable, confident, and powerful, regardless of what happens. It's your brain and your mind, and you can think any thoughts you want to. Never let anyone tell you that you are less than great.

Decide how you will turn your negative thoughts into positive reinforcers. _____

_____

☐   Once you've figured that out, check the box on left.

Become More Self-Reliant

By developing more self-reliance, you'll learn that you can depend upon yourself in increasing amounts.

This brings self-confidence. That means taking the time to learn to affirm yourself, learning to handle finances, learn to take care of your house, car, or clothes. Learn to do things for yourself. Sometimes going on back-packing or outdoor ropes-and-challenge courses can build this self-reliance.

What one thing can you do tomorrow to be more self-reliant? _____

_____

☐ Once you've decided that, check box on left.

Conquer Your Five Biggest Fears

These fears will vary from person to person. But when you face these fears head-on and deal with them, you can develop a tremendous sense of self-confidence. Here are the ones that I thought (past tense!) were important.

- fear of dying
- fear of losing love
- fear of failing
- fear of public embarrassment
- fear of marriage

To conquer those fears, I purposefully set about doing things that forced me to grow and deal with my doubts, insecurities, and fears. By handling them, I have gained a tremendous amount of peace about life and increased my self-confidence.

List your three biggest fears.

_____

_____

_____

Name one thing you can do to conquer each fear.

_____

_____

_____

☐ When you have written out your fears and what you can do to conquer them, check box on left.

Value Your Vitality

This is a tremendous self-confidence builder. Learn to take great care of your body (stretching, aerobics, and weight training three to five times a week); learn to eat well (low in fat, plenty of fruits and vegetables); and learn to keep your personal energy high (breathing, water, activity, and attitude).

Realize that you are important and equal to anyone on this planet. The truth is, no one is more valuable or less valuable as a human life. Some behave badly, but their life is still human. Some behave wonderfully, but they're not God. Learn to respect your time, your values, your dreams and yourself.

You have many values; list three here.

_____

_____

_____

☐   Check box on left when you have finished.

Learn to Express Your Creativity

Creativity is a terrific source of self-confidence. Why? Because it feeds the heart and soul to continually see your own forms of expression out in the world. Your work may be through music, writing, art, dance, singing, crafting, pet shows, theater, cooking, painting, building, designing, or gardening. But the more types and the more variety of things you create, the more you get to express yourself. And the mere expression of yourself can provide great feedback (of course, a royalty check wouldn't hurt, either!)

What is your special way to express yourself?

_____

If you don't have one, what form of expression could you develop that would make you happy?

_____

_____

☐   Once you've jotted down three ideas, check box on left.

Learn to Avoid Trouble

Sometimes trouble comes in the form of certain people. You know who they are. They bring you nothing but grief. They lie, they might have a big mouth, they might stir up others, but the bottom line is that they make your life miserable. You also need to recognize the most common situations you find yourself in. For example, do you spend half your life trying to fix people who don't really want to be fixed? Get rid of negative, unsupportive people in your life who sap you of energy, make negative comments, and make you miserable. You'll miss them for about ten minutes. Then you can go on with really living your life.

Who, if anyone, in your life is bringing you grief?

_____

If this individual is not a positive influence, why do you keep this person in your life?

☐   Once you've determined you need to make changes, check box on left.

Get Help

Be honest with yourself. Tell the truth. If you have any persistent problems in life, get professional help. These problems are a continual drain on your self-confidence. They could be as simple as a minor health problem or as significant as counseling for depression. Get the help you need.

In all honesty, is there a problem you need help with? Reach out to those professionals who can help.

☐   If you've made a decision, check box on left.

Give Back to Others

The more you give to others, the more you develop communication, poise, and self-confidence. Become a tutor, give time to charity, develop an apprentice program. Take the time to help someone else that needs it. You'll grow and so will they.

In your daily life, take the time to do an unexpected kindness for another. Write it here.

_____

☐   Once you've thought of one and recorded it, check box on left.

Read Extensively

One of the great ways to build self-confidence is to stay informed. Know about your areas of interest, learn about general areas, explore things that the opposite sex might be interested in. With no excuses, set aside the time each day to grow! Its not unusual to read 10 books and 25 magazines in about four months. Everyone likes to know what's happening—it feels good to be in the know!

Set aside 15 to 20 minutes each day to read something other than schoolwork. What will you read tonight?

_____

☐   Once you've decided, check box on left.

Learn to Ask Better Questions

Just by itself, asking questions can help boost self-confidence. But by asking the right questions, you can do the following:

1. Get another person interested in you personally.
2. Acknowledge another person. Most people will feel flattered and proud that you asked for their expertise.
3. Learn something you did not know before, either for commercial gain or for the love of learning.

What are three questions you can use to get to know someone better?

1. _____

2. _____

3. _____

☐   List them and check box on left.

Cultivate Integrity

There are things that you can do to cultivate integrity. First, keep your word. You'll feel good about yourself when you tell the truth. Then be sure to do what you say you'll do. If you make a promise that you can't keep, communicate that to those who can do something about it at the earliest possible moment. They will feel they can trust you to follow through. Because many people don't keep their word, it will set you apart. Being special and feeling special are just some of the many fringe benefits of being a person of integrity.

What makes you a person of integrity? _____

_____

Give an example of something that reflects your integrity. _____

_____

☐   Check this box when you have answered.

Review

Once you have finished this, today's assignment is completed. Before you close the book and move on to something else, let's review what you accomplished.

✓ You learned about self-esteem.
✓ You determined three things you can do to boost your self-esteem.
✓ You discovered how important choices are for your life.
✓ You found out how to build your self-confidence and translate it into success.
✓ You became acquainted with new and exciting things about yourself.
✓ You read your review for the day (that's this list).

 Congratulations! You have completed Day 17 of your 30 days. Close the book and we'll see you tomorrow!

Day 18

 Check-in
Did you finish yesterday's chapter? If not, get to it. Then start here.

HANDLE PERSONAL PROBLEMS

Research by Dr. Antonio Damasio (Iowa State University) and Dr. Joseph LeDoux (State University of New York) suggests that our emotions affect our critical thinking skills, decision making, and creativity. We all have problems, but personal problems can either be a positive lift or a black hole. It's up to you. What makes the difference is how you *respond* to your problems. Dealing with them positively has a great deal to do with getting better grades. Here are five secrets to handling personal problems right away.

Five Secrets

1. First, tell the truth about the problem. Think it through, talking about what happened. Try it from many points of view. Don't try to look good, don't try to justify it, and don't blame anyone. Just tell the truth. If you aren't sure of the truth, go ask a close friend or start keeping a journal to help you sort out the truth.
2. Separate people from the problem. Don't say, "Jeff was being a jerk!" The truth is that Jeff did

something, and you *decided* he was a jerk—that's an opinion, not a fact. Say, "Jeff took my books and I was ticked off!"

3. Be supportive of others. Other people may not know how to deal with their problems. Be a strong listener. Be empathetic. You don't need to be supportive of stupid behaviors, but you can still support your friends. You'll need that support some day, too.

4. You be the one who takes the first step to solve a problem. Others may be too scared, too busy, too proud, too embarrassed, or may lack the skills or guts. You be the one to ask, "Is there anything I can do for you to make this better?"

5. Problems always have a price and a reward. If you walk away from a problem, it's always temporary. However, most problems keep recurring until you solve them once and for all. You'll learn which kinds those are. Only a few problems are like skateboards that you can just hop off of.

The worst problems are like a freight train jumping the tracks. It is out of control for a while, but eventually it comes to a stop. And what's left to do is clean up the mess it made along the way. The bigger the problem, the longer it will take to sort out the mess. When you've done all you can to solve the problem—you've told the truth and accepted your part of the responsibility—you just may need to be patient. When things are at their worst, say to yourself, "This, too, shall pass." The pain may be heavy, but the pain will go away. Those concepts will give you a good starting point. Now, what do you actually do?

Five Steps to Success

The easiest way to deal with problems and conflicts is to use the OTFRC concept. You might use the saying, "On the friendly road to Chicago" as a way to remember the letters, OTFRC. Those letters stand for this five-part process:

1. Observe. State your observation. Just the facts only. "You said that you'd call me last night."
2. Thoughts. Tell the other person your opinions about the facts. "It was thoughtless and flaky to not call."
3. Feelings. Share your feelings about what happened. "I felt disappointed, worried, and hurt. I was mad at you, too."
4. Responsibility. Tell the other person what part of responsibility you played in the scenario. "I'm wondering if it was something I did. Maybe I didn't give you my number. Maybe I didn't tell you I had to wait up for you and keep others in my family off the phone."
5. Contract. What do you want to happen? What is the agreement that you want for the future? "Can we make a better arrangement for the future? Let's agree on whether you might call or definitely will call ahead of time. Maybe we can agree on a time slot. For instance, if you can call, it'll be between 8 and 8:30 P.M. Is that a deal?" It sounds a bit formal, but you get the idea. Make it your idea and use your words, just keep the same basic concepts.

Now, start today with these five steps to solve any biggie in your life.

☐ When you've read the preceding section, check this box. You're one step closer to your goal!

TIME MANAGEMENT SECRETS

You're no different from everyone else. Rich or poor, happy or sad, brown or black or white, everyone gets just 24 hours in a day. The difference is in how you manage those hours. Time can't be managed; time management is just an expression. What you need to do is *manage your activities*.

First Easy Step

Every day make sure you know what's important. You'll only know that if you set goals. Set short-term and long-term goals. Those were part of the first week's assignments in this program. Now is a good time to back up and check in on those goals you set. Do you want to change them? Or do you need to make any changes in your strategies to reach them? Make sure that you do that today, no matter what.

First, learn to say No to things that you really don't want to do. It could be a special event, traveling out of town, lunch, or just hanging out.

If you can gain just one hour a week for the next four months, you'll have that extra advantage you need to get better grades. All it takes is being clear on your priorities, so you know when to say yes and when to say no. Name something that you've been saying Yes to, that

you're now going to say No to: _____

_____.

♦ Keep phone calls to just five minutes. Make your calls early. That way you can leave a message for others if they're out. Call instead of writing a letter when it's faster or better to call.

♦ Make decisions promptly (as soon as you have all the information). Handle your papers the fewest number of times possible.

♦ Keep your study area clear. Phone ahead when you have appointments or need to pick things up—you can get directions and confirm that everything's ready.

♦ Keep lots of healthy quick snacks—like carrots, apples, bananas, water, and fruit juice—around your apartment, dorm, or house. Only hang up clothes that are ready to be worn again. Plan your clothes a week in advance.

♦ Plan, plan, and plan some more. What has to get done, no matter what, today? Always have a priority for the day. Make a plan and follow through. Use note paper or computerized calendars.

- ♦ Are there times you can do two things at once? Do you have something to do while waiting in lines? Do you have something to do while you're waiting for things to cook, things to be returned or fixed?

- ♦ Keep asking yourself the question, "What's the best use of my time right now?" Then map out a few strategies to get you going. Get up ten minutes earlier than you usually do. Jot down things that could save you time.

- ♦ Remember that satisfaction comes from how many tasks you *complete*, not how many you *start*.

- ♦ If you can think of ways to better manage your activities, write them down here:

_____

_____

_____

_____

_____

_____

☐   When you've read the section above, check this box. You're one step closer to your goal!

Review

Are you finished with today? Great! Before you close this book and move on to something else, let's review what you accomplished.

✓ You made the decision to continue the program.
✓ You read the check-in statement.
✓ You learned five steps to handle personal problems.
✓ You discovered that you can say no more often.
✓ You realized that you can manage your activities smarter.
✓ You read your review for the day (that's this list).

 Congratulations! You have completed Day 18 of your 30 days. Close the book and we'll see you tomorrow!

Day 19

TEST-TAKING STRATEGIES

Success leaves clues! Students who get A's and B's have discovered or invented a system that works. Naturally, the system that works for one student may not work for you. Some methods work most of the time. The strategies listed here will work for you all the time.

Step 1: Begin Today!

Get familiar with chapters way ahead of where you are in class. Browse; look at pictures, illustrations, problems, and other visual aids. It is not only easy to study things you don't have to, but it also lays the foundation for future learning. This method is called preexposure.

Ask questions in class. Your goal is to get B's and A's right at the beginning. That way, the professor thinks you are a top student and is biased towards you from now on. You will have a good reputation after just one test! What kinds of tests are given? Do they ask for lots of detail, or just basic ideas and themes? Is creativity encouraged, or is the class run by the rules? Exactly what should assignments look like?

STRATEGIES

Build a relationship with your professor early in the semester so the professor makes positive associations between you and learning. This shows a genuine interest in learning as opposed to quick fixes at test time.

Step 2: Strive for Long-Term Learning

Your brain has both short and long-term memory. Short-term memory involves activities such as looking up a phone number, dialing it, and then forgetting it. For tests at school, you need long-term memory.

Try to study at least five minutes a day in every subject, even if you have no assignments. The review will help lock the material into your long-term memory.

Know exactly what will be tested. If you are unsure what will be on a test, ask now, during the class, instead of waiting until test time. The highest scores will go to the students who know the most about the exam, not those who know the most about the subject.

Ask the professor for a second or alternative suggestion for reading material. Sometimes a second book or article is easier to understand and it can make better sense out of a tough subject.

Use class time to study and get ahead. If the instructor strays from the subject, make use of that time! Later on, you'll have less to do and your review will make more sense.

Be aware of the school's resources. These days, nearly every community college or university has free or cheap tutoring available. Find out about it from the student center and take advantage of it.

Step 3: Get Focused Close to Test Time

Find out what kind of test will be given. If it's objective (true/false, matching, fill in, multiple choice, or sentence completion), use the memory techniques and concentrate on details. If it's more subjective (essay or opinion questions), learn themes. Choose five or ten main themes and learn enough about them to write on each. Study chapter headings and subheadings from your text.

Ask the professor if any old tests are available to study. Surprisingly, sometimes they are available. This will help you understand the style, amount of detail, and contents of the upcoming test. Ask former students of that professor or class about the kinds of tests used.

Join a study group or review session with A or B students, but not with C or D students.

Read your notes out loud. Record key points on a cassette tape and play them back. The best time to listen is when you awaken in the morning. The mind is very receptive at that time.

Make up test questions. As you figure out the most likely questions, you'll start to think like your professor and become better at anticipating test questions. Make up your own and practice writing answers for them.

Identify what you don't know. The best students figure out what they don't know, and that's what they study. Use the index at the back of your textbook and review each entry that falls within the pages you are studying. If you don't know much about a term or concept, look it up, learn it, and then write it down. After each term you learn, review the index again for others you need to learn.

If you are confused, get help. Ask classmates, parents, tutors, professors, or professors' aides. Visit places, such as museums, exhibits, or movies. Go to the library and find another book on the subject that is easier to understand.

Study in short blocks of 20 minutes each. After each 20 minutes, get up, stretch, and have a drink of water. You'll stay fresher longer, understand more, and learn faster.

Put key ideas, hot tips, and easily forgotten terms on 3″ × 5″ cards. Reduce information to a few key words; add symbols and pictures for graphic reminders; use color. Make flash cards with key facts on one side and questions on the other side. Carry these cards around with you two weeks before a big test. Any time you're in a line or have to wait somewhere, pull out your cards and study them.

Cram—it can help! Your brain remembers information learned in the beginning and the end more than that learned in the middle. Cramming comes near the end of your study process. If you have been doing your coursework and going to class, you'll be able to build on what you have worked over time to learn. If you have done nothing for an entire semester, still cram, but don't expect it to make up for what you've missed.

Step 4: Boost Your Attitude

Keep up your positive attitude right before the exam. Tell yourself that the test is just a shopping list of information that the professor designs. It's not that different from a list you'd make up for the grocery store, but instead of shopping for food, you're shopping for information.

Prepare your body. Make sure you get six to seven and a half hours of sleep the night before your test. That's because your brain has approximately 90-minute sleep cycles. When you wake up in the middle of a cycle, you feel irritated and unrested. When you awaken at the end of a sleep cycle, you feel rested. If you want to get up at 7 A.M., go to sleep at 11:30 P.M.

Go for a walk, exercise, or play a sport to speed your metabolism, lower your stress, and boost your enthusiasm. Eat healthy foods with a high water content, such as fruits. Eat only a small amount of easy-to-digest food; if you eat too much, your body will be sending its energy to your stomach instead of to your brain. Immediately before the test, eat a piece of fruit, because it gives your body fruit sugar (fructose) for alertness and energy.

Super cram. Minutes before the test, glance at your notes and relax. Studies show that doing mental warm-ups for the brain improves test scores.

Bring plenty of supplies, such as an extra pen or pencil and any required texts or papers. Be prepared for the possibility of an open book test.

Avoid negative pretest talk with classmates. Only join in a conversation that will boost your confidence. If it's a bunch of scare talk, leave the group quietly.

Arrive at class several minutes early to get your seat. Sit close to the front of class so you can ask questions of the professor more easily. Mentally rehearse your memory cues, your mind maps, your notes. Get into a lean-and-mean, test-taking monster frame of mind. Close your eyes and imagine yourself succeeding on the test. Take a deep, slow breath and sit up. Remember that no matter how well you have studied, there may be some questions you simply don't know. Relax—you'll do fine.

Step 5: Pass the Test with Ease

When you get the test, take another deep breath and relax. Then do the following:

Listen for instructions before you do anything.

Immediately write out on scratch paper or the answer sheet any key formulas, words, names, or dates. Take another slow, deep breath.

Scan the entire test. Read the directions carefully. If you are unsure of either directions or questions, ask your professor. By scanning all the questions first, your mind begins to figure out answers in advance.

Relax, focus, and figure out your attack plan. A low stress level keeps circulation to your brain flowing. Figure out your allotted time and how much time you can spend on each question. If there are 40 questions to answer in 30 minutes, that's little more than half a minute per question. Work quickly and neatly—neatness always counts, regardless of what the professor says.

Start with one or two of the easiest questions. That will boost your confidence and get your brain on track.

Give each question your best guess, and answer every question as you go. If you have time to work on it, great. If you get it right, great. If you don't, great—you gave it your best try. When in doubt, your first impresson is usually correct. Put a light, erasable mark next to the questions you don't know and return to them later if you have the time.

Think out your answer before you write it down. You may need to read some questions twice and rephrase or reinterpret them to make sure you are answering them correctly. Watch for critical words like *show* (give evidence), *contrast* (describe how something is different), and *compare* (tell how something is similar).

If you get stuck, move on. Breathe slowly, stretch your arms and legs, or get a drink of water if it's allowed. Close your eyes and picture your notes.

Never, ever cheat. Losers cheat. Liars cheat. Cheaters cheat. You are a winner. You are an honest person. You are a top student, whether or not the report card shows it yet. Your integrity is worth more than any grade. Every time you cheat, it does three bad things:

1.   It means you broke the rules, so you're guilty and have to cover it up.
2.   It causes you to think you can't get good grades the honest, fair and legitimate way, so it lowers your confidence and self-esteem.
3.   It makes you feel bad about yourself.

True/False Questions

♦ Look for limiting words like a*lways, never, all, every, should,* and *must.* Statements with these words are likely to be false. However, generalization words like *often, most, usually, rarely,* and *sometimes* are often used in statements that are true.

♦ The longer the statement, the more likely it is to be true. True statements usually require more words to narrow down meaning.

Multiple-Choice Questions

◆ Read the answer choices first. This way you will know the possibilities ahead of time, prepping your mind for the right one.

◆ Look for key words like *why* (which tells you to look for a cause). Watch for qualifiers, such as, "all of the following are true *except* . . ."

◆ Avoid thinking that multiple-choice answers should be balanced. If you have chosen three B answers in a row, don't start thinking you're due for an A, C, or D answer—don't look for patterns.

◆ Choose an answer that has the same singular or plural word as the question.

◆ Avoid creativity. Provide what the professor is looking for. This is no time to be cute, funny, or to express an opinion.

Sentence Completion

Make sure your answer follows logically from the question. Read it back to yourself to hear whether it sounds right. Use the length of the blank and number of blanks as a clue to the answer. When in doubt, guess— never leave a question unanswered.

Math Tests

◆ Use a pencil and scratch paper. When unsure of what a question means, draw out what you understand of it. Underline key words in the questions to make sure you answer them properly.

♦ If you definitely don't know the answer, make an educated guess. Use your common sense.

♦ Estimate your answer, then compare it with the one you ended up calculating.

♦ Exaggerated or long answers are usually wrong.

♦ Work backwards. Pick a possible answer and do the problem in reverse to find out if that answer actually works.

♦ Make sure your answer shows the same unit of measure that is asked for.

♦ Guess if you're unsure, especially in geometry. You can usually come close to the right answer just by using the drawings provided.

Essay Tests

♦ Organize your thoughts on scratch paper, if it's available. Read over all of the questions before you write about any of them. The most common styles of questions are the following.

  – *compare and contrast* (similar and different, good and bad points)
  – *trace the development* (over time, who, where, what, how)
  – *explain why* (give causes and effects)
  – *describe and discuss* (tell all you know, analyze the parts)
  – *develop* (trace a path over time leading to a conclusion)

– *outline/sketch/summarize* (describe key features, be concise)

– *criticize and evaluate* (judge the worth, justify your reasons)

♦ Choose essay questions you can succeed with. If you have specific knowledge, do the ones that require that knowledge. If you don't, answer the ones that are more open and give you some leeway! These require less specific recall of dates, people, and events.

♦ Keep track of time. Give yourself a time limit for each part of your essay—the outline, introduction, main section, conclusion. Check your watch and stay on track. If you catch yourself running out of time, quickly outline your remaining key points. You may get quite a bit of credit for just doing that.

♦ Write as much as you can on the topic, but keep your words, sentences, and paragraphs short. Professors want to see how much of the right things you know, but do not want to read a cumbersome essay, for which you may get marked down. If you can't spell a word, use another one instead.

Write in this format: introduction, background, main points, conclusion. Begin with the same words used in the question itself and keep to the point. Include any applicable key facts you can remember.

♦ Neatness or sloppiness forms the first impression. If your paper gives the impression that a lot of care went into the production of it, it also appears as though care went into creating the content of it.

♦ Use strong statements. Let's say you're a political science major. Avoid vague or weak statements such as, "I think Clinton may have been stronger in foreign affairs than he was given credit for." Or, "I believe that the Gulf War was a big lesson," or "I suspect that civil rights issues will go on and on." Instead, say, "The reasons pundits say Clinton was not skilled at foreign affairs were . . ." Or, "Civil rights will remain an issue because of these five reasons . . ."

♦ Always write an answer even if you are not sure. Sometimes writing something will trigger your thoughts, and more will follow.

If you know nothing about the questions posed, invent a question that you do know something about, and write on that. In a note at the top of the essay tell the professor that you have studied and want to show that you have learned a lot. Although you are blanking out on the specific question asked, you would like him to consider partial credit on your essay. Often you'll get it.

Step 6: Last Chance!

Review all of your answers. Check the wording. Eliminate careless errors. Erase any smudge marks. Pause and think. Turn the test over, close your eyes, and relax. Let your mind fill with random thoughts. Sometimes you will think of new things in this quiet, restful mind-set. Better now than later on when the test is gone. Stay until the professor collects all tests, so if an answer comes to you, you can make a change.

Step 7: Learn from Your Test

When you get back your test, celebrate your success. If you didn't get the grade you wanted, find out why. Did you study the wrong thing? Did you study the right thing but forget it at test time? Were you unable to make sense out of what you knew? If so, find a student who did well and ask to see her paper for ideas on how to do better next time. Ask the professor for recommendations, too.

Look for patterns in your returned tests. Find out what kind of mistakes you made. You may have made just three different kinds of mistakes, but made them repeatedly on 15 different questions. Or you may have made the same mistake 15 times. That means you only need to correct one thing for next time! Get help. Never wait and hope things will improve on their own. They won't. Have the attitude that you are already an A student—you just want the test scores to prove it.

☐ When you've read the preceding section, check this box. You're one step closer to your goal!

BIRDS OF A FEATHER

The old expression "birds of a feather flock together" means that things that are alike tend to hang out together. What does that have to do with getting good grades? A lot! Students who get top grades think differently than those who don't. They are not smarter, but they have a different attitude, a different set of beliefs, and a different approach to school. You have to start thinking like an A student, because you're becoming one faster than you think. If you're not thinking like A students, find out how they think. Get to know some of them.

First Easy Step

First, locate two or three top students in each of your classes. Then pick the one you feel the most comfortable being around. Learn exactly what makes him an A student. This habit is called modeling.

Modeling applies to every facet of life. If you wanted to become a successful musician, you wouldn't hang around lousy musicians—you'd hang around the best ones you could find. If you wanted to become an athlete, you'd hang around the best ones you could possibly find. If you wanted to become a successful business person, you'd hang around the best one you could find.

Modeling works, because you learn by observing, listening, and asking questions. It's one of the best ways to learn to be an A student! Here are the two steps to modeling the mind-set of the A students you meet:

1. Be genuinely interested in them. Be friendly. Introduce yourself. Find out where they're from. Ask where they went to school before the one they're at now. Ask how much they study. Do they read much? Do they have much free time? Do they have a life?

2. Figure out what could work for you. Once you get a chance to develop a friendship or even just a passing acquaintance, take stock of what have you learned. Are there tips or strategies that you can apply? If so, when will you implement them?

☐ Check this box if you have already done this. If not, when will you make the time to begin using these strategies?

Write the day and time you'll begin here: _____
Good job! A journey of a thousand miles begins with the first step.

Review

Once you have finished this, today's assignment is done. Before you close the book and move on to something else, let's review what you accomplished.

✓ You made the decision to continue the program.
✓ You read the check-in statement.
✓ You learned some better test-taking strategies.
✓ You figured out what methods you can use.
✓ You made a promise to meet a couple of A students.
✓ You read your review for the day (that's this list).

 Congratulations! You have completed Day 19 of your 30 days. Close the book and we'll see you tomorrow!

Day 20

 Check-in

First, did you complete yesterday's chapter?
If so you're probably smarter already! Now you
can do the fun weekend stuff.

REVIEW AND SNEAK PREVIEW

Remember one week ago when you did a photoflash
sneak preview of this whole book? Today you will do it
again. Simply take a look at each page for the shortest
length of time you can (one to two seconds, like a
photoflash!). Let your brain absorb as much or as a little as naturally happens in that time. Use a relaxed, soft

PHOTOFLASH

focus with your eyes, purposely not trying to read anything. At one second per page, this entire book (all 30 chapters) will go very quickly.

You'll continue doing this one more time (in seven days). By the end of the course, this same exercise becomes a powerful review. And it will take very little time, too. Go ahead and photoflash every page in this book. That's all you will do today. Turn pages and glance at them.

☐   When you're done, check this box.

Review

You have finished for the day! Great job! Before you close the book and move on to something else, let's review what you accomplished:

✓ You made the decision to continue the program.
✓ You read the check-in statement.
✓ You photoflashed the whole 30-day program.
✓ You read your review for the day (that's this list).

 Congratulations! You have completed Day 20 of your 30 days. Close the book and we'll see you tomorrow!

Day 21

 Check-in
First, did you finish yesterday's photoflash review? Pretty amazing, wasn't it?

FREE DAY

As usual, today is your personal free day. Kick up your feet and do a little jig. Go enjoy yourself! Get some fresh air, create some fun, make cookies, or just lounge around. Compare notes with your study buddy, or catch up on your reading.

Today is the day to catch your breath and de-stress. So relax, NOW!

Review

Once you have finished this, today's assignment is over. Before you move on to something else, let's review what you accomplished.

✓ You made the decision to continue the program.
✓ You read the check-in statement.
✓ You figured out what you want to do for fun today.
✓ You read your review for the day (that's this list).

 Congratulations! You have completed Day 21 of your 30 days. Close the book and we'll see you tomorrow!

Day 22

✔ **Check-in**

First things first. How are you doing? Have you finished yesterday's chapter? If not, get to it as soon as you can (before you start today).

WINNING SPEECHES

Most students dislike giving speeches or oral presentations. In a way, that's good. Why? It's good because it's a skill that others often fear or do poorly—that makes it something you can learn to do well so you'll stand out in a positive way. All you need is the formula for preparing and delivering a winning oral presentation every time and some practice. Here's the seven-step formula.

1. Start with an idea.
2. Shape your idea.
3. Gather information.
4. Structure it.
5. Rough it.
6. Buff it.
7. Get feedback.

Step 1: Start with an Idea

All speeches start with an idea. Your idea must meet three criteria.

♦ Is it appropriate—is it what was asked for?

206

- Is it defined enough—not too big or too small?
- Can you gather enough resources for background material?

If you don't have a topic, try these three approaches.

- Ask your professor, friends, or classmates for ideas.
- Brainstorm on paper by writing ideas, related ideas, and ideas those ideas remind you of.
- Browse in a book or magazine, or watch a few minutes of TV.

Step 2: Shape Your Idea

Now do word association. Write every related word you can think of on your brainstorming visual map. You can sort out the value or depth of the topics later. Let's say you were assigned a topic on brain research. Your brainstorming might look like this.

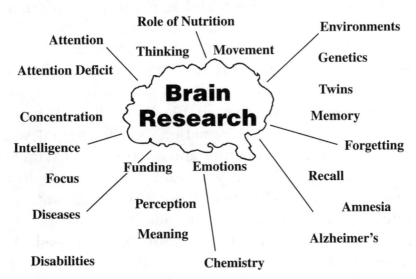

Make sure your topic isn't too big or too vague. What you have now is way too broad, but it's a good start. It was just brainstorming. Now, you'll choose just a small area of brain research. It might be what's new in funding or intelligence building. Let's say you were brainstorming topics in history or politics. The growth of the civil rights movement in America is too big a topic. Narrow it down—maybe by examining an event and the role it played, or the role a particular individual, such as Malcolm X, played.

Next, map out some of your ideas for your talk. Use the mapping technique described in the section on note taking. Write your topic in the center of a blank page and circle it. Let's say you're a psychology major. Your class is Introduction to Brain Research. Then start selecting and narrowing down some of your topics.

Step 3: Gather Information

Learn to search quickly and accurately for information for your speech. You've got three libraries to choose from. In your home library, check for any books, newspaper or magazine articles, TV specials, or movies. If you're a computer user on the Net, use a Net browser service to get some ideas or details on-line. At your school library, ask the information desk for help if you need it or go to the computer and do a search. Chances are good you'll find what you want. You can also do a search at your local public library. You may want to photocopy pages or articles relevant to your topic.

Collect more sources than you think you'll need. On one side of a 3″ × 5″ card, write out the source, author, date, place, publisher, edition, and pages that you could use. On the other side, write out key ideas, quotes, statistics, and examples.

Step 4: Structure It

Now that you've gathered some content, start thinking about what you'll bring to the speech. What's your opinion or bias on the developing theme? All speeches need a theme and a certain style. Adopt a point of view and think about an interesting angle to your topic. Give it life and pizzazz. You need to know all of the categories your information fits into. Look at these guidelines for structure and think about how you would structure the information mapped out below.

1. Introduction (10 percent of speech)

    ♦ Grab the reader's interest with an unusual story or shocking statistic.

    ♦ Introduce the topic: talk about how much of it you'll cover and the point of view you'll take.

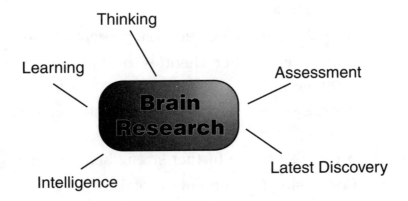

♦ State the importance of the topic, its timeliness, its impact.

♦ Tell why you chose this topic. Draw the interest of the listener. Be excited and enthusiastic. Passion is the key!

♦ Summarize your key theme or main thesis in a clear, concise statement.

2. Background (20 percent of speech)

♦ Give a brief history of the topic; be interesting and stick to the point.

♦ Explain any key events, special people, or terminology.

3. Main Body (40 percent of speech)

♦ State important information and key arguments.

♦ Limit arguments or ideas to three or fewer.

♦ Use accurate, strong, passionate language.

♦ Present arguments in order from strongest to weakest, from least controversial to most controversial.

4. Strengthen Your Position (20 percent of speech)

♦ State any other theories or opposing viewpoints.

♦ Assess their strengths or weaknesses (find their flaws).

♦ Build a case to further strengthen your ideas.

5. Conclusion (10 percent of total speech)

♦ Restate your theme and opinion

♦ Introduce no new ideas.

♦ Be extra clear and concise.

♦ Conclude with a motivating and positive statement.

Step 5: Rough It

You already have the key ingredients to start writing a rough draft. You have the topic, the angle or theme, the background information, and a structure for it. For your draft you can either use a computer to create cue cards or you can use index cards. On your computer, you can simply divide up the speech into the same five sections as those listed on page 212.

The alternative to a computer draft is a stack of blank 3″ × 5″ cards. You will later assemble your speech from these. Title your cards to correspond to each of the five parts of your talk. On the back of the cards, write out some key phrases to help you remember what you want to say. Do not write your talk word for word. It's too much work; there's no payoff for it; it'll sound stilted and unnatural; you'll feel too stressed trying to memorize it.

Step 6: Buff It (Final Touches to Make It Great)

♦ Rewrite your key ideas for the presentation on index cards. The rewriting helps you learn it and gives you a chance to make the words more meaningful. Use key words as triggers for the rest of the words that won't be written down. Use color, symbols, and pictures to jog your memory.

♦ Memorize, word for word, only the first and last sentences of your speech—this gives you confidence and certainty.

INTRODUCTION
CARD

My attention getter:
My theme or thesis:
The scope of my talk:

BACKGROUND
CARD

Why it is relevant now:
Who should care:
Key vocabulary:

MAIN BODY
(TWO TO FOUR CARDS)

Three to five points
Keep them simple and clear
Strongest first

STRENGTHEN
YOUR POSITION

Rebuff what any opponents
have said or might say

CONCLUSION
CARD

Restate your case
Be clear and compelling
Be passionate!

◆ Practice doing the oral presentation. See where the weaknesses are. Make corrections on your note cards or on the computer.

◆ Use props or visual aids. Use something that will bring extra pizzazz to your presentation—sound effects, an object, a chart, or some other visual aid that is applicable and easy to understand. Write or tape key words on your props for even greater recall. It reduces your nervousness and grabs audience attention.

◆ Involve the audience. Ask questions. Ask them to demonstrate something for you. Set up something with another student who can react or have some interplay with you.

◆ Right before your speech, get mentally prepared. Picture yourself making a successful presentation, practice your gestures (make them big!), and give yourself a pep talk.

When it's time to give your presentation, breathe deeply and relax in front of the room. Smile; make eye contact with the friendly faces. Then give your opening statement and keep going. If note cards are permissible, use them. If not, use the memory tips listed in Day 10 to memorize the key points. Use the notes taped to your props. End on a positive note and thank the audience.

Step 7: Feedback—Learn from Your Speech

Wait—you're not finished yet! Get feedback from your professor so you'll do better next time. Ask how you did in these specific areas so you'll know where you can improve or what you did well.

A SUCCESSFUL PRESENTATION

- *Introduction:* how was it?
- *Body of speech:* how was your content?
- *Interest:* did you keep audience's interest? If not, what could you do differently next time?
- *Gestures, posture, and use of voice:* need improving?
- *Props used:* were they useful or distracting?
- *Examples:* was your speech colorful and relevant?
- *Conclusion:* did you have a definite and strong ending?

You can practice making speeches when you talk to your friends, your parents, or to classmates. You can practice in front of the mirror, with a tape recorder, or outdoors by yourself. Successful public speakers will tell you that the main way they became good at speaking was by practicing and getting feedback, again and again. The more speeches you make, the better you'll get, so stay with it!

☐ When you've read the preceding section, check this box. You're one step closer to your goal!

KEEP A BIG WHY IN YOUR GOALS

You've already set your goals, so you know *what* you want, but you need a reason to reach your goals. You need a *why*. A strong *why* will fuel, drive, and motivate you to reach your goals automatically. The *why* can be positive or negative. Most people use both: "I'd better get my car fixed so I'll have it ready for the weekend. If I don't, I'll feel like an idiot."

First Easy Step

First, write out everything positive you'll get by reaching a goal you've set. (For example, you might get feelings of success, accomplishment, or pride; you might gain self-confidence or self-respect; you might get a better job or be able to graduate). These are the positives. Write in your own four personal *whys*—or positive reasons —for reaching this goal:

1. _____   2. _____

3. _____   4. _____

OK—you've given your brain the carrot, or the positives; time to give it the stick, or the negatives. The desire to avoid pain or embarrassment is a great motivator. Write down all the bad things that could happen if you don't reach your goal. (For example, you might feel let down or embarrassed; be mad that you wasted your time; be depressed; not graduate; get a low-paying job; have to hang out with loser friends.) Write down the negatives—the *or else* reasons—for reaching your goal:

1. _____   2. _____

3. _____   4. _____

Now, just to make sure that everything makes sense, do this: Read your original goals from the beginning

(Day 1). Follow each one with the word *because*, and then complete the sentence with your eight reasons—four positive and four negative. Here are examples of four of them.

➤ I am getting A's and B's in at least three subjects in 30 days because it will boost my self-confidence.

➤ I am getting A's and B's in at least three subjects in 30 days because I want to graduate and get into graduate school.

➤ I am getting A's and B's in at least three subjects in 30 days because I am sick and tired of low grades and I deserve better.

➤ I am getting A's and B's in at least three subjects in 30 days because life's too short to be a loser.

This seems like a simple exercise, like one that won't make much difference. But remember, your brain is driven by emotions, passion, and strong reasons to do something. We'd like to believe we're solely driven by logic, but recent brain research tells us otherwise. Once you have a really strong reason to get A's and B's in 30 days, you'll find a way to get it done. Good luck!

☐ When you've read the preceding section, check this box. You're one step closer to your goal!

Review

Today's assignment is done. Before you close the book and move on to something else, let's review what you accomplished.

✓ You made the decision to continue the program.
✓ You read the check-in statement.
✓ You learned how to prepare and deliver a great oral presentation.
✓ You discovered why the reasons behind goals are important.
✓ You added a few extra *whys* to your goals.
✓ You read your review for the day (that's this list).

 Congratulations! You have completed Day 22 of your 30 days. Close the book and we'll see you tomorrow!

Day 23

JUST SHOW UP

It's simple. When you go to class regularly, you never miss anything. This doesn't mean that every class will be a four-star, Siskel & Ebert two-thumbs-up, Indiana Jones thriller. We all know class may not be the most exciting place on earth, but it's your job for now. Go to class because

- the professor sees you and knows that you are committed.
- it ensures that you never miss out on a thing.
- it keeps you in the habit of learning.
- even if you are a bit tired or sick, you'll learn more in class than in bed (unless you're really sick).

First Easy Step

To start, set a goal of 100 percent attendance. It's a great goal to have. Follow up by making a sign or poster for your study area. Here's what to put on it: *This is a 100 percent month!* Then do your best to make it one!

☐   Check this box if you read the preceding section. Now, get yourself some materials and make your 100 percent sign.

KEEP STRESS LOW

Stress has a bad name. Actually, *some* stress is good. It creates appropriate tension, anxiety, and worry over getting things done, which is useful. Too much stress is no good. You get irritable, don't think straight, and get sick because it depresses your immune system.

The Five Best Ways to Keep Stress Low

1. Work out every day. Do something physical. Researchers tell us that physical activity tenses, then relaxes the muscles, boosts the immune system, and lowers our stress. Try walking, biking, yoga, swimming, rollerblading, skating, playing a sport, working out at a gym, or anything that uses the muscles and boosts your heart rate for 15 to 20 minutes.

2. Learn to say *No*. You don't have to say Yes to every idea, every event, every party. Say it gracefully so your friends understand that it's nothing personal, that you just need some down time. If they want you to join them to just hang out, have an answer ready: "Hey, thanks, but I'm booked and gotta run!"

3. Get organized. You'll feel less stressed if you have a place in your room for everything. You'll also feel less stressed when you have commitments written down on a calendar or date book. Then you'll know what you can say yes to; your decision will be based on reality, not fear. When it comes to school, plan your work and work your plan.

4. Tell the truth. You'll never have to lie to cover up another lie. You'll be able to sleep at night knowing you are an honest and good person who keeps your word. You'll feel better about yourself and others will like you for your genuine character.

5. Learn to do what's really important to you. Stress skyrockets when you are doing things you don't want to do or things you don't have time for. Always set aside the time to do what you love to do—maybe it's music, working out, talking to a friend, or a hobby.

First Easy Step

Study the five stress reduction steps just listed. Do one of them today; do the rest over the next four days. Be relentless. The number one cause of illness is stress. Do you get colds or the flu frequently ? Getting sick can hurt your grades. If you want top grades, you've got to be well enough to produce. Get a handle on stress today. Do one stress-buster now!

☐   Check this box if you've assessed your stress level. If you need to do something about it, write down your next step here:

REMEMBER THE CHEESE

"Remember the cheese" is an expression about reaching goals in life. An experiment was done with rats in a maze. The researchers put a piece of cheese at the end of the maze to reward the rats who found the correct path. After a few false starts and trial runs, the rats learned the correct path and went down it alone for the cheese. When the cheese was moved, it only took the rats a couple of trials to discover that the cheese was gone, and they took another route. So far, so good.

The experiment got interesting when they made cardboard life-size mazes for humans. The researchers put a $5 bill at the end of the maze. Soon the humans got good at getting to the end of the maze to get the reward. Then, just as with the rats, the researchers moved the goal. The new subjects, college students, kept going down the same path, insisting that it was the correct one. They insisted they were right. In fact, months after the experiment was ended, college students broke into the lab at night trying to find the $5 bills! But the cheese (the reward) was gone. What happened?

Sometimes life changes. People change. Directions change. It can get confusing on the path to your reward—B's and A's. There will be plenty of distractions, but are you big enough to deal with them? No matter how a professor, a school, a parent, or a friend affects things, your goal should stay the same. If something you are doing is not working, change it, do something different. Don't get stuck like the students in the experiment. Keep your eyes and ears on the goal.

First Easy Step

Analyze how you are doing today in regard to your goals. If you're on track, keep doing what you're doing. If not, make the changes needed to get to the reward. Nobody is interested in your excuses, justifications, or reasons. The only important question is, "Did you get the cheese?" And if you've been following directions so far, the answer should be "Yes!"

☐ Check this box if you've evaluated your path and your success so far. If you need to do something about it, write down your next step here:

_____

Review

Are you through? Before you close this book and move on to something else, let's review what you accomplished.

✓ You made the decision to continue the program.
✓ You read the check-in statement.
✓ You realized the value of attendance.
✓ You read five ways to keep your stress low.
✓ You learned the concept of going for the cheese.
✓ You read your review for the day (that's this list)

 Congratulations! You have completed Day 23 of your 30 days. Close the book and we'll see you tomorrow!

Day 24

 Check-in

It's time for a progress report. How are you doing? If you are caught up, go ahead and start here.

STUDY SHORTCUTS

Have you ever heard the phrase, "Well begun is half done"? That's how it is with studying—half of the ordeal is getting started. You've already learned some study skills earlier in this book, so this chapter is just to give you a few shortcuts. If studying on a daily basis will give you the B's and A's you want, you need to learn how to *start* studying every day. Let's make it a habit. This routine is a sequence of things to do to get your brain in the study frame of mind.

First Easy Step

1. Remember, this is just a way to create a study routine—a pattern you'll be doing from now on.
2. First, you'll leave the room, then come back into it, fresh.
3. You'll go up to a book on your desk, tap it and say, "It's easy!"
4. Then tap this book twice and say, "This is the system!"
5. Then point to yourself and say, "I'm the person!"

6. Then stretch, take in a few deep breaths, and exhale slowly.
7. Then sit at your study area and say, "Now's the time!"

This method works because it is designed to get your mind, body, and soul ready to study and achieve serious results. Go ahead and try it. It takes about a week to start having the best effect, so start now.

You've already learned the full-blown study method two weeks ago. This is not a repeat but a different way of looking at the same strategies. Here are simple, study shortcuts that have been proven successful with thousands of students. Let's say you have only 35–50 minutes to study a long chapter, or several chapters, or to study for a big exam. Get yourself a watch and follow this method by the numbers.

Step 1: Clean the Scene (two minutes)

♦ Clean your study area and remove any distractions (phone, roommates, for example).

♦ Gather your study materials/supplies.

Step 2: Get Set, Mind-Set (five minutes)

♦ The mind-set you want is "Yes! I'm ready to study! Yes! I'm going to nail it down! Yes! Studying is easy! Yes! I have the tools I need to succeed!" If you are not in this mind-set, read the chapter on motivation (Day 15). Whatever you do, never study unless you're in this psyched-up, power-study mind-set. It's a waste of time if you aren't fully focused and motivated.

♦ Set a time limit. The brain works best with deadlines. Your goal might be a certain number of pages in 20 minutes, or a chapter in 30 minutes. It might be to correctly answer the study questions at the end of the chapter. Figure out how much time you have, how much material you have to study, and set a goal.

It's tough to set a goal unless you really understand the assignment. Make sure you get it right. If a professor says, "Study Chapter 5," that means very little, unless you ask some questions. "What should I focus on?" "How well do I need to know it?" Put your goal on a sticky note and put it on the wall or a lamp near you.

Step 3: Preview, Ask, and Map (five minutes)

♦ Preview the materials. Find the section or chapter that you'll be studying. Browse through and study the graphics. Look at titles, headings, subtopics, pictures, charts, examples.

♦ Ask yourself key questions: Still browsing (not reading), spend a half a minute per page, find boldfaced headings and ask questions about each one. These should be questions you think the professor might ask, or questions you think you need to know to understand the material. Basically, the questions are: Who? What? Why? When? Where? and How?

Your goal is to prime the pump: to stimulate, excite, and activate the brain towards more curiosity. By asking questions, you've set up unfinished business for your brain. You've got it thinking about those questions and the possible answers. Asking the right question is probably the single most powerful tool you can use for better comprehension. How do you know the right question to ask? You don't. You experiment and ask a lot of them. The more you ask, the more you are likely to ask the correct one.

♦ Map out key points on a mind map. Use color; add pictures. Make this skeleton overview fun to look at. Refer to the chapter on note taking (Day 5). Put the title of the chapter or section in the center and circle it. Then use the chapter subheadings (up to 15) for your branches. Fill in the branch titles using alternating colors. You have now given your brain a map of the key points of that chapter.

By creating this map of the material, you've learned a lot already. By asking questions, you have identified exactly what you need to know. Look at it, close your eyes, and visualize it. Alternate looking and visualizing until you can picture your map vividly. Now, instead of having to plod through your textbook slowly, you simply need to go back through your chapter or section and gather the answers to your questions.

Step 4: Gather the Goods (15 minutes per session)

♦ Write as you read. You'll be doing two things. First, you'll be going back over the material with the intention of answering the questions you asked earlier. Don't read every word or try to get deep information. Simply find the specific answers to the specific questions you asked. The answers you find may be important class or test information, so write down the key points on your mind maps. Second, you accomplish an additional goal of studying for a future exam while you read.

♦ Go as quickly as you can and complete your chapter or section. Gather the answers and write. If you need a study break, get up, stretch, drink some water, take a few deep breaths, and have a seat again. Stay focused, stay in a power-study state, and keep going.

♦ Study in short bursts. The brain learns best in pulses and cycles. The material at the beginning and end of a lesson are most readily remembered. So have more beginnings and ends and less middles. The secret is to study in 15 to 30 minute cycles. When the time's up, go for a two-minute walk, have a drink of water, and stretch a bit. Then, go back and review the notes.

Step 5: Reality Check (10 to 20 minutes)

Find out what you know and don't know. You've now gone over the material three times—first to familiarize yourself with the structure and get a mental map, second to ask key questions, and third to gather key information and answers to your questions. That's usually enough to give your brain a thorough understanding of the material. However, it's always best to double-check your understanding, so do the following:

♦ *First, check your visual map.*

If you can look at it and talk from it, that's a good start. You should be able to explain all key words on your branches. If not, go back to the sections in the book and review them. The point of a mind map is not to duplicate the book, but to trigger your memory of the material.

♦ *Second, check the table of contents.*

Look up key phrases and subtitles from the book. Can you talk about the ones that you are supposed to be learning? If so, great! If not, go back to that section and learn it. Then add those key bits to your mind map.

♦ *Finally, check the index.*

If your chapter went from pages 50 to 70, go to the index and check all words that have page numbers between 50 and 70. If you know the words, great! If not, look them up and add them to your mind map.

Step 6: Activate the Learning (5 to 20 minutes)

Now's the time to transfer the learning from short-term to long-term memory. You know the ways you like to learn best. Pick just two of the five steps below. By activating the learning, you are ensuring long-term retention and a better grade at test time.

1. Talk it through with a study buddy or in a study group.
2. Close your eyes and picture the mind map with all its key points.
3. Stand up and act it out with your body.
4. Mind map it again.
5. Make a rap: talk out the key parts, or read key facts or ideas aloud to music.

Step 7: Seal the Deal (5 minutes)

This is the step that not only instills the material in your memory, but also gives you the confidence to get an A on the upcoming test. Follow the steps listed below and enjoy the positive results.

♦ Memorize key parts and intensify the memory by repetition.

♦ Put key ideas (with drawings or pictures) on 3″ × 5″ cards. Use them like flash cards and review often.

♦ Review all material again within ten minutes, 48 hours, and seven days.

♦ Preview the future; mentally rehearse success on the test. See yourself being relaxed, confident, and doing well.

☐   When you've read the preceding section, check this box. You're one step closer to your goal!

POSITIVE QUESTIONS

USE THE POWER OF POSITIVE QUESTIONS

Your ability to stay positive while studying has much to do with your ability to ask the right questions. Your brain is always asking you questions and your brain is always answering them. If you say, "I hate studying!" the question your brain just answered was "What's wrong with studying?" But if you asked your brain a different question, you'd get a different answer. At study time, then, ask yourself the question, "How can I learn this quickly, thoroughly, and still have fun at it?"

Some questions are useful, but others are a dead end. Dead-end questions are negative, depressing, and a waste of time. Here's an example: "Why do I always blow it on tests?" You're not really an idiot, but your brain will probably tell you, "You always blow it on tests because you're an idiot!" So start asking your brain useful questions instead of dead-end ones. A more useful question would be, "What have I learned about test taking that will help me on my next test?"

First Easy Step

First, start listening to your comments and opinions—especially when it comes to school, grades, and learning. Any time you say something negative, stop yourself. Ask yourself a more useful question. Instead of "What went wrong?" ask yourself, "What needs to happen to make things right? Second, get quick practice by changing the three questions written below from dead-end ones to useful ones.

Dead end: Why does this professor always give us so much homework?

Useful: How can I get through these assignments fast and still do well on them?

Dead end: Why do we have to learn this stupid stuff?

Useful: What can I do to make better use of my time? Or, How can I make this more interesting?

Dead end: How come this assignment takes forever to do?

Useful: How can I complete my assignment faster?

POWER OF POSITIVE QUESTIONS

Dead end: Why does all this have to be so boring?

Your rephrasing: _____

_____

Dead end: How come I got a lower grade than I deserved?

Your rephrasing: _____

_____

Dead end: Why do my parents have to be on my case all the time?

Your rephrasing: _____

_____

Learn to make this a habit. Positive questions are very powerful. They have the capacity to transform an ordinary or boring experience into a dynamite learning session. To get into this habit, do it once, then repeat again and again each day.

☐   If you are willing to make this a new habit, check this box.

Review

Once you have finished this, today's assignment is done. Before you move on to something else, let's review what you accomplished.

✓ You made the decision to continue the program.
✓ You read the check-in statement.
✓ You learned a simple get-ready-to-study routine.
✓ You found out about some quick study strategies.
✓ You discovered the power of positive questions.
✓ You read your review for the day (that's this list).

 Congratulations! You have completed Day 24 of your 30 days. Close the book and we'll see you tomorrow!

Day 25

 Check-in

Ready for some more great grade-boosting ideas? If you're ready, start here.

EIGHT WAYS TO BE SMART

Dr. Howard Gardner of Harvard University says that we each have eight intelligences. An intelligence is a way of expressing what you have learned. You might express it by solving problems, singing, building, writing, or making something. If you have difficulty learning something in one intelligence, simply use another. For example, if you don't want to read a book, you might want to get a video on it, listen to a lecture, create a rap, design a project, or interview others on the topic. Here are the eight ways to learn.

1. **Verbal/linguistic.** Listen to audiotapes, hear a lecture, make a tape, or do a rap. Talking and listening, writing or describing.
2. **Bodily/kinesthetic.** Act it out, play a role, build a project, do a dance, or play a game. Do something that lets you get your body into it.
3. **Interpersonal.** Study with a friend, partner, family, buddy, or work in a team. Talk to others, ask questions, learn by listening and discussing.

4. **Spatial.** Use the brain booster miniposters, make drawings or mind maps, or visualize. Move around; study in different places.
5. **Logical/mathematical.** Reasoning and thinking skills, problem solving, organizing, sequencing, predicting, and analyzing.
6. **Musical/rhythmic.** Listening to music, making a rap, humming the words, tapping while you think it out.
7. **Intrapersonal.** By yourself—writing in a journal, setting study goals and reaching them, reflecting and doing the 30 success habits.
8. **Naturalist.** Ability to find, isolate, identify. and sort things. It's how you construct relationships and patterns.

Which of the eight ways to learn do you like to use the most? The more ways you use, the more ways you have to succeed. Experiment and use several of them. Learning can be creative, easy, and fun!

Figure out which eight kinds of smart you are. List the

ones at which you are strongest _____

_____   _____

Question: How can knowledge of your strengths help you succeed?

Answer: You can use your strengths to compensate for any weaknesses. After all, to be successful in life you don't need to be good at everything, just the things that are important.

LEARN TO USE THE AS IF ATTITUDE

The *as if* frame of mind and body means that you act *as if* you are already the person or *as if* you already have the skill that you want. For example, how do A students study? Are they confident, positive about their future? How much time do they spend studying? Where do they spend their time at school? With professors? With D and C students? In the library? Where do they go for help when they are stumped? If you don't know how an A student thinks, walks, sits, breathes, and lives, you ought to know!

First Easy Step

The next time you sit down to study, use the *as if* frame. Study *as if* you were a straight A student. You'd be confident, assertive, relaxed, and absolutely sure that you could master the material in the least time possible. In fact, study *as if* you're a genius. You may get the results you want!

☐   When you've read the preceding section, check this box. You're one step closer to your goal!

MANAGE YOUR EMOTIONS

For good or for bad, your emotions run your life. What you are upset with, in love with, excited about, runs you. Generally, those who can manage their emotions can manage their lives. Here's an example. A friend promises something. He doesn't keep his

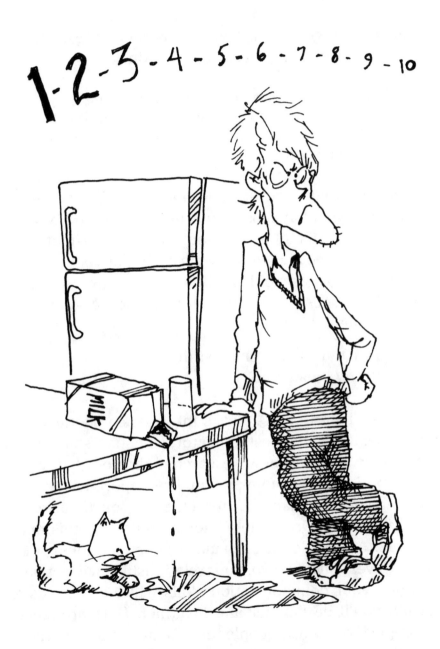

HANDLING STRESS

promise. You get angry. Your day is ruined. How much better it would be if you started thinking,

> The promise is not being kept *so far.* Life goes on. There's probably a reason for it. I'll deal with it when I have to. At worst, this could become an inconvenience.

Quit making a catastrophe out of everyday events. No matter what happens, take a deep breath, relax, and move on. Be thankful that you are healthy—that you have eyes to see and ears to hear, and that you live in a country that has schools and the opportunity to better yourself. Promise yourself to follow the two-step formula for mental health:

1. Don't sweat the small stuff.
2. It's *all* small stuff.

You've heard of I.Q. That's intelligence quotient. At one time, it was the best indicator we had of someone's smarts. But today, new research indicates that your *emotional* intelligence may be more important to your lifelong success than I.Q. In fact, the book *Emotional Intelligence* by Dr. Daniel Goleman tells why this may be true. As you learn to manage your emotions, your stress level will go down, your relationships will get better, and your communication skills will increase. As a result, you'll be happier and healthier. Here are some examples of ways people can better manage their emotions:

♦ Learn to handle Distress—that's when you have too much stress.

- Be smart about when and how much attention you give to things and people.
- Know how to develop rapport with others.
- Know how to make good decisions.
- Learn how to manage negative self-talk.
- Learn skills to deal with loss and grief.
- Try to see and hear yourself as others do; that's self-awareness.
- Communication skills: Can you share what you want in the way you want, or do others misunderstand you often?
- Conflict resolution and upsets: Do you know how to deal with frustration and anger?
- Relationship skills are important, too. Do you know how to make friends with strangers? Can you maintain school and personal friendships over time?

Most of these skills have already been introduced in bits and pieces throughout this 30-day program. This is not supposed to be a course on emotional intelligence, but at least you can begin to be aware about it. Let's address one of the topics: how to deal with anger or frustration.

First Easy Step

First, recognize when you are angry or frustrated. That's the first step to mastery. When you do experience an emotion that you don't like, try these four strategies:

1. Talk to someone about it. You might talk to a best friend, a parent, a relative, or sometimes to a stranger—someone you meet in line, in a store, or in the library. The main thing is to talk it out with a good listener.

2. Ask better questions of yourself. Change your focus of attention! Ask yourself questions such as:

> What's funny about this that I haven't thought of?
> If I were 90 years old, how would I react to this?
> If I wanted to keep my peace of mind, what would I do?
> What other responses could I have that would be healthier for all involved?

3. Physically move! Get up, sit down, take a deep breath, dance, go for a walk, shoot baskets, ride a bike, swim, skateboard, surf, exercise, do anything!

4. Learn something from mistakes. If something goes wrong, instead of blaming others, ask yourself, "What could I have done differently?" Maybe next time you'll be able to avoid the bigger or more painful mistakes.

Now think of the last time you lost your temper, and plan what you could have done differently. Then think about the next time you might lose your temper. Plan what you're going to do, and think about how good you'll feel after managing your emotions. Write your answer here:

☐   Once you've done that, check this box.

Review

Once you have finished this, today's assignment is done. Before you move on to something else, let's review what you accomplished:

✓ You made the decision to continue the program.
✓ You read the check-in statement.
✓ You learned the eight kinds of smart.
✓ You discovered the power of the "as if" frame of mind.
✓ You understand better the power of your emotions.
✓ You read your review for the day (that's this list).

 Congratulations! You have completed Day 25 of your 30 days. Close the book and we'll see you tomorrow!

Day 26

 Check-in

First, did you complete yesterday's chapter?
If not, get to it as soon as you can. Then start today's chapter.

HOW TO WRITE A RESEARCH PAPER

Writing a paper, whether it's three or 33 pages is rarely fun, but it can be much easier than most students make it. You may have had a bad experience before or maybe no one ever taught you an easy way to do it. This chapter shows you, step by step, how to produce the

best paper you are capable of writing. You'll learn how to make your paper organized, how to make it flow, and how to present your material for maximum results.

Pick a Topic

You need an idea for a starting point. You'll either be assigned a topic or get to choose one on your own. To find your own, sort through your textbooks or notes, or go to the library and do some exploratory research. There are endless sources for ideas.

➤ on-line databases through providers like AT&T, CompuServe, or America Online (AOL)

➤ newsletters; consult *Newsletters In Print*

➤ borrow, purchase, or use CD-ROMs from a media center

➤ *World Book, Collier's,* or *Encyclopedia Britannica*

➤ specialized encyclopedias (like *Afro-American Encyclopedia, Jewish Encyclopedia, New Catholic Encyclopedia, Encyclopedia for World Art,* and *New International Wildlife Encyclopedia*)

➤ public libraries, public interlibrary reference loans

➤ your friends, relatives, their parents, and community members

➤ university and college libraries

➤ museum or exhibit libraries

➤ magazine articles; use the *Guide to Periodical Literature*

➤ almanacs; *The World Almanac and Book of Facts* and *The Information Please Almanac*

Choose a topic you like, one that you're interested in learning more about. Once you've picked a possible topic, determine whether or not it's the right one for you. Can you tell if it's going to be too narrow or too broad? Does it have some controversy to it? Timeliness? Is there a sufficient number of sources of information about it? This helps you make a smart decision.

If You Are Assigned a Topic

When a professor suggests or requires certain books, there's a reason for it. If it's unclear, ask the professor what he or she has in mind. Just knowing why you're using a particular book can make it easier. If a professor suggests a particular author or topic, take it seriously. It's not worth putting a lot of work into a project only to find out later that the work was not really what was wanted. Often times you get caught between wanting to learn what you want to learn and having to do what is asked for by the professor.

Have a Take

A take is a point of view, an angle, an opinion. As an example, doing a paper on the growth of the civil rights movement in America would be a major undertaking. However, if you focused on the key roles, positive or negative, of the minister Louis Farrakhan, you'd have a narrower topic and a possible point of view. The next step in shaping your ideas is to begin a rough outline. Include only main or key ideas in this preliminary outline. Draw a mind map. Start with your topic in the center and make branches coming out of it like the spokes of a wheel. Put different areas you want to talk about on different branches. Then you can see how many subtopics you have and how much information you can expect to generate for each of them.

Research It

The best place to begin research is the library. Ask a reference librarian or someone at the information desk. The best path might be the World Wide Web or the Internet. Check a general index to magazine articles, such as *The Readers' Guide to Periodical Literature*, or appropriate specialized indexes such as the *Humanities Index* or *The New York Times Index*. Do an on-line bibliographic computer search for your topic, if your library has this service. Use other reference books, such as encyclopedias and bibliographic publications that are available for many subjects, to locate what might be important sources.

Be sure to use the most recent publications so that your research provides the reader with the most accurate and up-to-date information. Either store it on computer or list each source on a separate 3×5-inch index card. Include author, title, publisher, date and place of publication, edition, card catalog number, pages used, and your comments about the appropriateness of the source (e.g., core source, borderline source).

Mark your source index cards with a notation to reference any especially key source. On the back of each 3 × 5-inch card, put any key ideas from the material. That way, you'll only need to look up a source once, unless it's one of the few that you decide to study in depth later. In general, try to spend only a few minutes on each source before moving on to the next.

Browse Through Your Materials

Browse through your materials first. Start to get a feeling for your topic and to form opinions about the focus of your paper. Ask yourself qustions like these:

♦ What are the main elements of my topic?

♦ What are my feelings on this?

♦ What do I want to focus on in my paper?

♦ What does the professor expect from my research?

Make Sense Out of It

Now you're ready to begin a structure; it's your paper's skeleton. Do this before you start adding the flesh to your writing. Your paper will have several predictable sections.

♦ **Introduction** Grab the reader's interest with an unusual story. Introduce the topic to the reader—its scope, width, and direction. State the importance, timeliness, and impact of the topic. Tell why you chose the topic. Summarize your thesis in a clear, concise statement. Motivate or tantalize the reader to read on.

♦ **Background** Give a brief history of the topic—be interesting. Briefly introduce other areas of your topic. Help the reader know what you know—key points only. Explain any terminology, key words, phrases.

♦ **Main body** State strongly and truthfully the evidence to support your thesis or viewpoint. Use accurate, strong language. Present arguments and ideas in an easy-to-follow order: perhaps from least to most controversial, or from strongest to weakest in reasoning.

♦ **Counter-argument and rebuttal** State any opposing viewpoints. Assess their strengths and weaknesses. Build a case to further reinforce your viewpoint.

♦ **Conclusion** Restate your thesis and your reasons for believing in it. Briefly walk the reader through your arguments and ideas. Analyze and evaluate your key points for the reader. Introduce no new information; restate prior ideas clearly. Conclude with a succinct and moving statement.

Get Out Your Journal

Your journal is a collection of notes you make as you finish reading/researching each day. Those notes will trigger your thoughts when it's time to write your paper, so you won't have to go back and reread. Keep this in either your computer or a notebook of lined paper.

Each time you finish reading, enter the date and the materials/page read. Then write two to five statements about what you read. Mention the key ideas and some minor ones, too.

Organize Your Information on a Visual Map

Gather all your materials: your journal of notes, the professor's exact instructions, colored pens and paper for a mind map (see Super Note Taking, page 49), and your sources. Then draw the mind map of your research paper.

Write Your Rough Draft

You have the first two key ingredients to begin writing: the background notes and the structural framework. How do you know how much to write on each section of the paper? One thing that may help you is to estimate the final length you want your paper to be. Then start assigning approximate page lengths to each part.

Introduction	5–10 percent
Background	10–20 percent
Body	40–60 percent
Rebuttal	5–15 percent
Conclusion	5–10 percent

For example, on a 20-page paper, your introduction might be two pages, background three pages, body twelve pages, rebuttal two pages, and conclusion one page. This is only a guideline. Your professor may have different standards. Check what the expectations are before you begin writing your rough draft.

Use a computer if you can; a typewriter is second best. Very few professors will accept a handwritten paper. Use the visual map to trigger your thoughts.

Now is the time to start writing. But instead of starting at the beginning, start on any part of the paper. Why? It's more important to get the ideas and words flowing. You can edit them later. Don't worry about grammar, sentence structure, or spelling yet. Just get it done. You might start with the section on background of the topic. The introduction is much easier to write after you have done most of the paper. Plus, the background familiarizes you with the material. The background is easy to state, easy to organize, and easy to say a lot about. After the background section is complete, move right on to the main body of the paper. Write for an hour at a time, then take a short break. As soon as you can, while you're fresh, go right back to it.

Keep the stream of thoughts coming and write as long as you're producing good material. If you get stuck, take a longer break and come back when you're rejuvenated. Some students can write well into the night and others do best in the morning, from about nine until noon. Just write when you're at your best and keep going until it's done. Then get away from it for a while. You'll have a fresh perspective when you come back to it.

Proof and Polish

After you have taken a break from your material, go back and read it aloud. It should read well, as if you were hearing a speech on your topic. Put in transition phrases where necessary. Make sure all the spelling is correct. Check for errors in logic and flaws in statistical data. Have a friend read the paper so you get feedback.

You're on the path of B's and A's, so its OK to need some help. Swallow your pride—it's no use asking for feedback if you don't accept advice! Finally, after revisions, give it one last reading out loud before you call it finished. If you like it, turn it in. If not, revise some more. Add stronger words (use a thesaurus) to increase the clarity or impact. Consult a handbook on style and usage to ensure that you have used the proper format for your paper and that your grammar is correct.

Documentation is critical to your success. A bibliography is no longer necessary by Modern Language Association (MLA) standards. You will simply list sources on a page called Works Cited. Make sure you have given credit where it is due, that you have either inserted quotation marks or set off any quoted material, and that you have given correct and complete references for your sources.

Double-check to ensure you have avoided plagiarism. Plagiarism is where you lift, take, copy, or otherwise steal someone's phrases, sentences, or paragraphs without giving credit to them. If you like what someone said, that's all right. Just remember you might be able to say it better or update it. If it's too good to change and you just use a couple of words, simply use quotes. Then make sure you identify the author. Being a good writer doesn't mean that you never use the thinking and writing of other people. It just means that when you do it, you do it in appropriate ways. As my wife Diane said, "You'd be surprised how flattered other writers are when they are mentioned in your books. Just make sure to give them credit."

Neatness Counts

Print out your paper double spaced, with half-inch margins on each side. Make sure that you number all the pages. Put your paper into something to protect it (like a file folder). You don't need a cover page unless your professor asks for one. Center the title and put your name under it. Also include the date, name of course and instructor, and any special designations your class may have. The new MLA standards say you can do all this on the first page.

Your final copy is expected to be printed on regular white bond paper. Make sure your paper is perfect in its presentation: no smudges, stray marks, or errors. The neatness of your paper does affect the grading, whether it's a conscious decision by the instructor or not. Be meticulous and rigorous in assessing the quality of your paper before you turn it in (on time!). If you follow all of these steps carefully, you'll have a good shot at getting an A.

When You Get Your Paper Back, Learn from It

If you got an A or a B celebrate! Then write down a list of what you did right. If you didn't get a high grade, what did the professor say you needed to do? Was it the content and topic? Was it following directions? Was it turned in late? Was it neatness and spelling? Write down the professor's feedback. Learn from it and correct your path.

One Last Strategy

If you didn't get the grade you wanted, tell the professor that you really want to get a B or an A, and that you'd like to redo your paper. Ask for your professor's suggestions and then ask whether you can do a revision. Fight for a better grade. The worst that can happen is you'll get turned down. Then you're no worse off than before you asked.

Regardless of what happens, learn from it. Above all, keep reminding yourself that you're a good person and a capable student. Just keep at it!

▢ When you've read the preceding section, check this box. You're one step closer to your goal!

Review

You made it! Before you close this book and move on to something else, let's review what you accomplished.

✓ You made the decision to continue the program.
✓ You read the check-in statement.
✓ You learned how to write a research paper.
✓ You read your review for the day (that's this list).

 Congratulations! You have completed Day 26 of your 30 days. Close the book and we'll see you tomorrow!

Day 27

FLASHBACK AND FLASHFORWARD

Here we are, the last chance for a photoflash sneak preview of the whole book. You remember this gives your brain great reviews of all the things you've learned. Plus, there are a couple of days left to preview.

PHOTOFLASH

By now, you know just how to do it. Simply turn the page, glance at it for one second or less, then look at the next page. This exercise has become a powerful review. You'll recall that it takes very little time. Go ahead and photoflash every page in this book. That's all you do today. Turn pages and glance at them.

☐   When you're done, check this box.

Review

All done? Today's assignment is, too. Before you close the book and move on to something else, let's review what you accomplished.

✓ You made the decision to continue the program.
✓ You read the check-in statement.
✓ You photoflashed the whole 30-day program.
✓ You read your review for the day (that's this list).

 Congratulations! You have completed Day 27 of your 30 days. Close the book and we'll see you tomorrow!

Day 28

FREE DAY

Relax, you're almost done. Today is a free day.

Do what your heart desires, or do your laundry (whichever is more pressing). Make important calls, go roller-blading, visit neglected friends, play a game of football, watch TV, laugh for no reason at all, or cultivate biological samples from the food left in your refrigerator.

Take a deep breath—you're almost there!

Review

How much of a review do we need for a free day? Not much. Go ahead and check it out.

✓ You made the decision to continue the program.
✓ You read the check-in statement.
✓ You figured out what you want to do for fun today.
✓ You read your review for the day (that's this list).

 Congratulations! You have completed Day 28 of your 30 days. Close the book and we'll see you tomorrow!

Day 29

 Check-in

First, did you enjoy your free day yesterday?
I hope so. Let's get started. We have just two more days.

LEARN THE WAY YOU LEARN BEST

Doesn't everyone learn the same? No way. If you know your best learning style, you can study more efficiently and effectively. You'll learn more, remember it longer, and enjoy the whole process—all in less time!

First Easy Step

You learn in three ways:

1. by seeing (reading, viewing films, and watching things)
2. by hearing (listening to lectures, music, study buddies, or audiotapes)
3. by doing (acting something out, or performing experiments in lab class, phys ed, theater, shop, and dance).

Which one's your favorite? Maybe you like a combination of the two; you might be *visual-kinesthetic*, for example (you like to see and touch). We all like each style at one time or another, but here's how to tell which is your overall favorite style of learning:

You are more *visual* if you spell, read, and visualize well; talk or respond faster than most; see pictures in your head; love watching people, things, and movies; use expressions like "see what I mean," "get the picture," and "from my point of view"; eat to live (instead of live to eat); like your clothes to match; like things neat; and don't mind noise.

You are more *auditory* if you spell poorly, talk to yourself, like hanging out with friends, use the phone a lot, recall lyrics to songs easily, dislike writing, dislike written or standardized tests, like the dialogue in movies, become distracted easily, learn languages easily, memorize in small steps, and raise and lower your voice often.

You are more *kinesthetic* if you learn best by doing; fidget a lot when you're not comfortabe in a chair; like to get up and move around; often feel hungry, tired, or energized; like action or emotional movies; dislike small-print writing; like computers; like to touch others while talking; are comfortable standing close to others.

Remember, your favorite way to learn might be a combination; combinations are quite common. Are you visual-kinesthetic—meaning do you first like to look at something, then go do it? Or are you auditory-kinesthetic—do you like to hear or talk about something, then go do it? Even though you use many ways to learn, one of these is probably your favorite. Once you figure out what is your favorite and your second favorite way of learning,

write them here: _____

_____

Now, what's your least favorite way?_____

_____

DRIVE YOUR OWN BUS

"Driving your own bus" is an expression that means being in charge of your own life. If others can pull your strings and jerk you around, then life gets pretty frustrating. But if you *choose* to react and respond in the way *you* want to, then life is a whole lot more fun.

First Easy Step

First, start identifying the ways other people and things cause you to react. If you get mad every time your roommate uses a certain tone of voice, you are the robot. You're the one that has lost the power to choose how your life goes. Your roommate didn't do it to you, you did it to yourself. If you run out of gas or spill a salad or get in a fight, guess who's to blame? Not the car. Not the salad. Not even the other person. Forget the word *fault*; start using the word *responsibility.*

Now that you've accepted responsibility, let other people know it. Change your words. Instead of saying "You made me angry," say "I felt angry." After all, no one *makes* you feel anything—you choose to feel the way you do. Sure, you've been brought up to feel certain ways about certain things, but you were brought up to use diapers and a bottle, too. You outgrew those, so how about outgrowing the other outdated and useless programming? Starting today, recognize blame messages; turn them into statements that prove you are driving your own bus!

☐ When you've read the preceding section, check this box. You're one step closer to your goal!

KEEP BALANCE IN YOUR LIFE

Balance means that you are taking care of all the important areas of your life at the same time. Balance means that you are not only healthy, but doing well in school and at home. It means that your relationship with your parents is strong and healthy. It means that you are balancing work and play, being social and independent. It means you are balancing your busy schedule and your stress levels.

You have time for friends and time for yourself. It does not mean that you have and do everything. It means that you have a balance of priorities in life. When you are out of balance, stress goes up, and you get down. You either get sick, depressed, or irritable. Who needs that? You don't.

Balance does two things for you. First, it keeps stress low, so you're healthier and happier. Second, it brings more satisfaction into your life. For example, if you only liked one food in all the world, eating would be pretty stressful—you'd always be worrying about getting that one food. And your satisfaction at eating time would be very limited. The more you enjoy—people, places, activities, and interests—the better your life!

First Easy Step

Give yourself a letter grade in each area of your life. If you get a C or lower start working to improve! You are an awesome person, and you deserve to have a rich, full life. But there's no free lunch—you have to work for it!

STUDY

PARENTS

PLAY

RELATIONSHIPS

FRIENDS

WORK

BALANCING

___ school	___ money
___ family	___ work
___ health	___ recreation
___ church	___ hobbies
___ relationships	___ friends

An area in which I'd like to improve is:_____

_____

These are specific steps I will take to improve this

situation: _____

_____

☐   When you have figured out what you'll do and
when you'll do it, check this box.

Review

Once you have finished this, you're about through
with this whole 30-day program. Before you continue,
let's review what you accomplished.

✓ You made the decision to continue the program.
✓ You read the check-in statement.
✓ You learned the ways you learn best.
✓ You understand the concept of balance in your life.
✓ You realize how important it is to drive your own bus.
✓ You read your review for the day (that's this list).

   Congratulations! You have completed Day 29 of
your 30 days. Close the book and we'll see you
tomorrow!

Day 30

REALITY CHECK

Wow! Hard to believe how fast time flies. It's been 30 days. You've done what you set out to do—learn the success strategies to get B's and A's in just 30 days. Now it's time for a reality check. Not a judgment day or grading time, just a check-in. Let's do a little research and find out the state of things. It'll take just a few moments.

Figure out where you are right now. You did this before, on Day 1. To make this fair to yourself, don't look back at what you wrote earlier. Let's check for progress. Please fill out the next section.

Name of Class (By its title)	Most Recent Quiz/Test (Within last 30 days)	Expected Grade (At course end)	Desired Grade (At course end)

Now, use this information to fill in the blanks on the next two lines:

Total number of classes _____

Number of B's & A's _____

☐   When you've read the preceding section, check this box.

PERSONAL PROFILE REVISITED

We did this before, but stay on this page and don't look back at what you put earlier. Let's check on progress. As before, tell the truth and circle your answer. Use 1 as the low end and 10 as the highest score.

On a scale of 1–10, how much do you like school? Circle your answer.

1	2	3	4	5	6	7	8	9	10
zip		low	average		not bad		good		excellent

What's your skill level in study skills and reading? Circle your answer.

1	2	3	4	5	6	7	8	9	10
zip		low	average		not bad		good		excellent

What are your confidence and self-esteem levels? Circle your answer.

1	2	3	4	5	6	7	8	9	10
zip		low	average		not bad		good		excellent

How do you rate your chances of finishing college? Circle your answer.

1	2	3	4	5	6	7	8	9	10
zip		low	average		not bad		good		excellent

Overall, how would you rate the way your coursework is going? Circle your answer.

1	2	3	4	5	6	7	8	9	10
zip		low	average		not bad		good		excellent

Good. Now let's go back to Day 1 and compare. Look at the scores you gave yourself then and the scores you gave yourself today. Take a moment and total up your scores.

NEXT STEP

Have you made progress? If you have, congratulations! Celebrate! Your next step is to continue to use these skills and apply them to keep your grades up.

Why Celebrate Successes?

Your brain remembers what brings it pleasure. It wants to do those things again and again. How did you celebrate the last time you got an A or a B? Have you planned the celebration for your next one? Positive emotion equals motivation for the brain, so reinforce your successes along the way.

First Easy Step

The next time you get an A or B (it's probably about to happen soon), celebrate! It doesn't have to be anything fancy, but do something!

♦ Try a simple cheer to yourself, pat on the back, a gesture.

♦ Indulge in a food treat: frozen yogurt, chocolate, etc.

♦ Call a friend and share the good news.

♦ Rent a movie/go to a movie.

♦ Recreation: swim, skate, bike, walk, surf, hike.

Go ahead. Make your plans! That A or B is just around the corner.

HOWEVER . . .

If you haven't made as much progress as you'd like, here are two suggestions. If you feel like you're on the right track, and you need more time to get used to the new skills, simply continue, starting on the days or chapters that you want more skill or knowledge in.

Otherwise, your alternative step is this: Do some soul-searching. Have you really done what each chapter asked? Have you stuck to the program day after day? Did you set goals? Did you invest 30 minutes or more a day? Did you browse all the chapters every day? If you answered no to any of these, you have some clues to what happened.

While very little is guaranteed in life these days, this 30-day program has been tested, with real-life students just like you. It works, but you have to work, also. You can still get the results you want. Take a minute and set some new goals. Figure out what you did that worked and what you did that you'll want to change. Make a plan for yourself and use tomorrow as the starting point. You deserve great grades. Go get them!

You Have Completed Your 30-Day Program

Go Celebrate!

BIBLIOGRAPHY AND SUGGESTED READING

Armstrong, William H. and M. Willard Lampe. *Study Tactics*, Hauppauge, NY: Barron's, 1983.

Barron's New Student's Concise Encyclopedia, 2nd ed. Hauppauge, NY: Barron's, 1993.

Buzan, Tony. *Radiant Thinking: The Mind Map Book*. London, U.K.: BBC Publications, 1994.

Buzan, Tony. *Speed Reading*. New York: Dutton/Plume, 1991.

Buzan, Tony. *Use Your Perfect Memory*. New York: Dutton/Plume, 1991.

DePorter, Bobbi. *Quantum Learning*. New York: Dell Paperbacks, 1992.

Dryden, Gordon and Jeannete Vos. *The Learning Revolution*. Torrance, CA: Jalmar Press, 1994.

Gelb, Michael. *Present Yourself*. Torrance, CA: Jalmar Press, 1988.

Goleman, Daniel. *Emotional Intelligence*. New York: Bantam Books, 1995.

Green, Sharon. *Making the Grade in College*. Hauppauge, NY: Barron's, 1990.

Howard, Pearce. *The Owner's Manual for the Brain*. Austin, TX: Leonorian Press, 1994.

Hutchison, Michael. *Megabrain*. New York: Hyperion Press, 1994.

Jensen, Eric. *Brain-Based Learning and Teaching*. Del Mar, CA: Turning Point, 1995.

Jensen, Eric. *Student Success Secrets*, 4th ed. Hauppauge, NY: Barron's, 1996.

Kenyon, Tom. *Brain States*. Naples, FL: United States Publishing, 1994.

Kline, Peter and Laurence Martel. *School Success*. Arlington, VA: Great Ocean Publishers, 1992.

Kline, Peter. *The Everyday Genius*. Arlington, VA: Great Ocean Publishers, 1988.

Lofland, Don. *PowerLearning*. Stamford, CT: Longmeadow Press, 1992.

Margulies, Nancy. *Mapping InnerSpace*. Tucson, AZ: Zephyr Press, 1991.

Mark, Vernon. *Brain Power*. Boston, MA: Houghton-Mifflin, 1989.

Markman, R. et al. *Ten Steps in Writing the Research Paper*, 5th ed. Hauppauge, NY: Barron's, 1994.

Paige, Michele. *After the SATs: An Insider's Guide to Freshman Year*. Hauppauge, NY: Barron's, 1991.

Pelton, Ross. *Mind Food and Smart Pills*. New York: Doubleday, 1989.

Porter, Patrick. *Awaken the Genius*. Phoenix, AZ: PureLight Publishing Co., 1993.

Rose, Colin. *Accelerated Learning*. New York: Dell Paperbacks, 1985.

Scheele, Paul. *The PhotoReading Whole Mind System*. Wayzata, MN: Learning Strategies Corporation, 1993.

Strunk, William Jr., and E. B. White. *Elements of Style*. New York: Macmillan, Inc., 1979.

Wurtman, Judith. *Managing Your Mind and Mood Through Food*. New York: Harper & Row/Perennial, 1986.

INDEX